Cragg Family Origins

Great Britain 1770-1859

David Cragg

Publisher: David Cragg

2016

This First Edition Published 2016

National Library of Australia Cataloguing-in-Publication entry

Creator: Cragg, David, author.

Title: Cragg Family Origins : Great Britain 1770-1859 / David Cragg..

ISBN: 9780994519207 (paperback)

Notes: Includes bibliographical references and index.

Subjects: Cragg family.

                Woolen and worsted manufacture--England--History--18th century.
                England--Genealogy.
                England--History--18th century.
                England--Social conditions--18th century.

Dewey Number: 929.20942

Cover Pictures

Top: "Keswick, Derwent &c. from the road to Kendal" engraved by J.Phelps after pictures by Thomas Allom, published in Westmoreland, Cumberland, Durham & Northumberland Illustrated, 1835

Middle: "Workington" engraved by R.Wallis after a picture by W.H.Bartlett, published in Finden's Ports and Harbours..., 1842

Bottom: Cockermouth: engraved by R.Sands after a picture by Thomas Allom, published in Westmoreland, Cumberland, Durham & Northumberland Illustrated, 1832

Contents

Dedicated to my father, Mervyn James Cragg (1932-).

Preface

When my grandfather, George Alfred Cragg, unexpectedly sent a letter to me in 1979, it was his kind way of helping me complete a primary school assignment. It contained the only information on the history of my ancestors I would have in my possession for the next 15 years. My grandmother, Edith, later commented that he enjoyed researching and writing it. The hand written letter detailed names and dates of four generations of Cragg family back to his own grandfather. That is where it mysteriously stopped. For many years, I wondered where the family had lived before arriving on Australia's shores. Still, as an 11-year-old, it was fascinating to pour over the letter and see dates that reached back into the 1800s.

In 1994, the opportunity to travel to the United Kingdom for a holiday arose. I had an inkling by then that the Cragg family had originated from England. With the help of relatives, I was able to discover immigration records, and consequently which county in England they had lived and worked in. The research went on from there for the next 20 years.

Whilst I was researching and writing, I often reflected on the numerous Bronte and Austen BBC period dramas, which I have consumed over the years. They gave some insight into every day rural English life during the late Georgian era and early Victorian era. However, I rather think my ancestors were more like the peasantry milling around in the background of a scene, rather than the privileged few in the foreground playing out a tragic or romantic tale. The real story is actually more complex, and the characters drawn from many historical sources. One aspect I have observed is the passing down of traits from one generation to the next. Not just physical appearance, but attitudes and inclinations. Resilience, civic justice, community, family and geniality are just a few common threads.

The towns of Keswick, Workington and Cockermouth have largely preserved their Georgian character, so it takes very little effort to walk through their streets and imagine ancestors going about their daily lives. To provide context to the characters, the history of the area and significant events that influenced their key life decisions and attitudes to life have been interwoven.

I would like to acknowledge the following people, without whose help this book would not have been possible. Colin and Winsome Archard, and Mervyn Towers. I am also indebted to J. Bernard Bradbury whose research into Cockermouth's past has been invaluable.

David Cragg - 5th great grandson of Isaac Cragg (1770-1858)
24 January 2016

Chapter One – Cragg, The Name.

The name CRAGG derives from the Gaelic 'creag', which in Middle English became 'crag(g)'. This name indicated "one who dwelled near a steep or precipitous rock or stone." Variants of the name include Craggs, Craig, and Craiggs. Other variants also exist that were the result of phonetic spelling from time to time. The earliest occurrence of the name found so far in England is Henry Crag in the Assize Rolls for Yorkshire in 1204. Later, in 1260, a Hudde del Crag appears in the Assize Rolls for Lincolnshire. In 1301, the Subsidy Rolls of Yorkshire contained references to Peter del Kragg and John Cragges.

In Scotland, John of the Craig (Johannes Del Crag) of Aberdeenshire led a party of 300 men into the Battle of Culblean, in 1335. John of the Craig was Laird of the Craig of Auchindoir (in the Parish of Auchindoir). Anneys del Crage of Edinburgh and Johan del Cragge of Lanarkshire rendered homage to John Balliol in 1296, and in 1323 reference was made to the land of James del Crag, son and heir of John del Crag, in Ayrshire.

It is difficult to ascertain whether these figures from history are ancestors or not of this line, but they are good examples of Cragg name variants. Only recently, in the late 1800's had the family name in Australia changed temporarily from Cragg to Craig.

A Family Crest?

It may come as a surprise that not every family has a coat of arms, or only a branch of a family has a coat of arms. A family member once granted a coat of arms passed it on to his descendants who had the right to bear that coat of arms. In England, the entitlement to bear a coat of arms is still tightly governed, as the Laws of Heraldry are still in force. It is difficult to say whether the Cragg family in Australia have the right to bear a coat of arms, as no direct link to an ancestor with a coat of arms has been discovered.

In the north-western English county of Cumbria (formerly Cumberland), there is a small farming village called Ireby. If you were to take the High Ireby Road out of the village and turn right into New Park Lane, you would find yourself driving down an old country lane weaving through paddocks full of sheep. Just past an old stone farmhouse, there lies an ancient stone church dating from Norman times (12th Century) surrounded by leaning tombstones and a metre-high stonewall. This is Ireby Old Chancel.

Figure 3 Ireby Old Chancel (David Cragg 1995)

Within Ireby Old Chancel, on the southern wall there is the following inscription upon a stone:

'George Crage, of Priour Hall Gent. who faithfullye served Queen Elizabeth, King James, Prince Henry and King Charles King of England 1626'[1],[2]

Figure 4 Stone Monument to GEORGE CRAGE

---

[1] Hudleston & Boumpherey, Cumberland Families and Heraldry, 1978.

[2] Paul Aubert Irby, The Irbys of Lincolnshire and The Irebys of Cumberland, Part II, 1939.

There is a shield accompanying the inscription on the centre panel of the monument that has 'ermine on a fess and three crescents'[3]. This shield has also been found in Greenford, Middlesex.[4],[5] Another shield of a different design originated from Devonshire. Interestingly the Shield (otherwise known as Blazon or Arms) is also that of Clan Craig in Scotland descended from the Craigs of Craigfintry (later Riccarton) which became a noted family.[6] Another shield of a different design associated with Cragg originated from Devonshire.[7]

Three crescents generally meant that this person was the third son. Prior Hall was owned by Carlisle priory and stood near the Ireby Church, but was demolished in the 19th century and moved to a location approximately a half mile north-east of the Church. The area previously known as Isaacby is now called Prior Hall.[8] The town of Ireby is only 15km north of where our Cragg family was located a century and a half later, in Cockermouth. Therefore, the coat of arms mentioned above may well be in the Cragg family. The full description of the coat of arms as known today in Burkes General Armoury is:

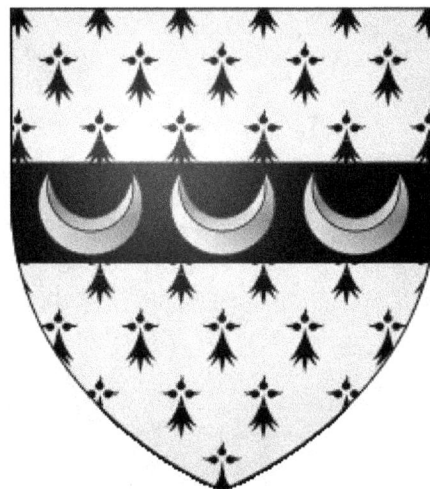

Blazon: Ermine on a fess sable, three crescents argent.

Crest: On a chapeau gules turned up ermine, a fleur-de-lis between two wings azure.

---

[3] Paul Aubert Irby, The Irbys of Lincolnshire and The Irebys of Cumberland, Part II, 1939.

[4] Hudleston & Boumpherey, Cumberland Families and Heraldry, 1978.

[5] The British Herald; Or, Cabinet of Armorial Bearings of the Nobility & Gentry of Great Britain & Ireland, from the Earliest to the Present Time, Thomas Robson, 1830.
http://books.google.com.au/books?id=c3EUAAAAYAAJ&dq=cragg%20heraldry&pg=PA332#v=onepage&q=cragg%20heraldry&f=false last accessed September 24th 2013.

[6] http://en.wikipedia.org/wiki/Clan_Craig, last accessed September 24th 2013.

[7] Hudleston & Boumpherey, Cumberland Families and Heraldry, 1978.

[8] Magna Britannia, a concise topographical account of the several counties of Great Britain, by D. and S. Lysons, 1816.

The motto of the Cragg family is *'bene merere et si praemia desint'*, which means 'he who serves reaps the final reward'. This is similar in sentiment to the motto of the Craig family *'vive Deo ut vivas'* which translated means 'Live to God that you may live'.

A Traitor in our midst?

King Henry VIII's reign is remembered for numerous notable events, from England severing its religious ties with Rome, to the execution of several of his wives during his quest for an heir to the throne. The dissolution of the monasteries by Henry under the guidance of Thomas Cromwell, which commenced in 1536, was a successful attempt to boost the royal coffers with the sale of Church land to English gentry. However, it also caused much ill feeling and distrust amongst the people of England. The Church had long been a source of comfort and alms to the poor, especially in the north of England where poverty was commonplace. Deeply rooted religious tradition had also been turned on its head. Little wonder the peasantry soon felt enough was enough when they saw Henry's new policy turn arable land into pasture and

Figure 5 Thomas Howard, 3rd Duke of Norfolk

tenements regularly knocked down in the process. The strengthening of royal control in the North not only caused peasant outrage, but fuelled resentment amongst the local feudal magnates as well. Many groups consequently formed at various locations in the North, generally banding together along traditional militia mustering lines. An estimated twenty thousand or more men, women and children took part in the rebellion in the North after having taken the rebel oath, in what became known as the Pilgrimage of Grace.

Thomas Howard, 3rd duke of Norfolk under the direction of Henry VIII capably suppressed the rebellion through a combination of threats and cajoling. While no pitched battle ever took place, the leaders of the rebellion were eventually captured and put on trial. In Cumberland and Westmorland, seventy-four men were singled out for execution on 24 February 1537. A letter from Norfolk to Henry VIII contained a list of men condemned to die at Carlisle.

Amongst them was a Richard Cragg of Eaglesfield (Richard Cragge of Eglesfyld) who had goods and chattels valued at £7 4s. 8d., which meant he was a well-to-do peasant possibly owning some land. Richard would have been hanged in his own village of Eaglesfield. If not executed there, then certainly in the town of Cockermouth. The bodies were to remain hanging from their gallows to provide a grim reminder to those who dared to challenge the authority of the King. However, the Duke of Norfolk wrote on 8 May that quite a few bodies including three who were hung at Cockermouth had been taken down by wives or relatives of the executed men. The village of Eaglesfield is located 1-2km southwest of Cockermouth, where the Cragg family resided 300 years later.[9] While no direct line to Richard Cragg can be established at this stage, it is possible he is related in some way primarily due to his geographical proximity to the Cragg line.

---

[9] Scott Michael Harrison, The Pilgrimage of Grace In The Lake Counties, 1536-7, Royal Historical Society, London, 1981.

Chapter Two - Background

Currently the lineage of the Cragg family can be traced back to the year 1770, in Northern England. Britain was unlike its European neighbours in many ways. It was this unique character, which had effectively prepared it for the bloodless revolution that would eventually sweep the world. The Economic Revolution brought forth changes in the Industrial and Social spheres of the British nation between 1760 and 1850. Britain no longer had the feudal system Europe still employed, and people who were not subject to poor relief were free to move about the country. Agriculture radically changed with land enclosure and new farming techniques, resulting in many tenant farmers leaving the land, or finding employment with the large landowners. Since the Glorious Revolution of 1688, the increasingly laissez-faire government effectively ruled the country. The monarchy was still intact, but had greatly reduced power. Thus profit making ventures and commercial expansion in trade, coupled with advances in technology (such as the steam engine) and a newly available workforce made the Industrial Revolution possible. People flocked from the country to the towns in search of work causing the urbanization of Britain. The population of Britain also increased rapidly due to the agricultural revolution and advances in health, reaching 9 million in 1801, from 6.5 million in 1750.[11]

Over time, England had been divided administratively into counties. The county that Cragg history is concerned with primarily is Cumberland, which was the most north-western county of England. On its northern border lay Scotland, while to its west the Isle of Man and Northern Ireland across the Irish Sea. To the east of Cumberland was Northumberland and moving clockwise the counties of Yorkshire, Westmoreland and Lancashire. Cumberland County was broken up along ecclesiastical lines into dioceses, though these dioceses were not always confined to the boundaries of the county. In 1770, the north of the county was the Diocese of Carlisle, with parts of Durham Diocese encroaching over the eastern border. The south of Cumberland was part of the Diocese of Chester. This has changed many times since 1770 and affects where certain civil and church records are kept today. Each diocese in turn was broken down into parishes, and each parish was served by a clergyman of the Church of England and

---

[1] Shena Coupe, Modern History, 1985, McGraw-Hill Book Company, Sydney.

a central chapel. The parish was also the smallest civil unit for administration, on which matters like poor relief were based.[2]

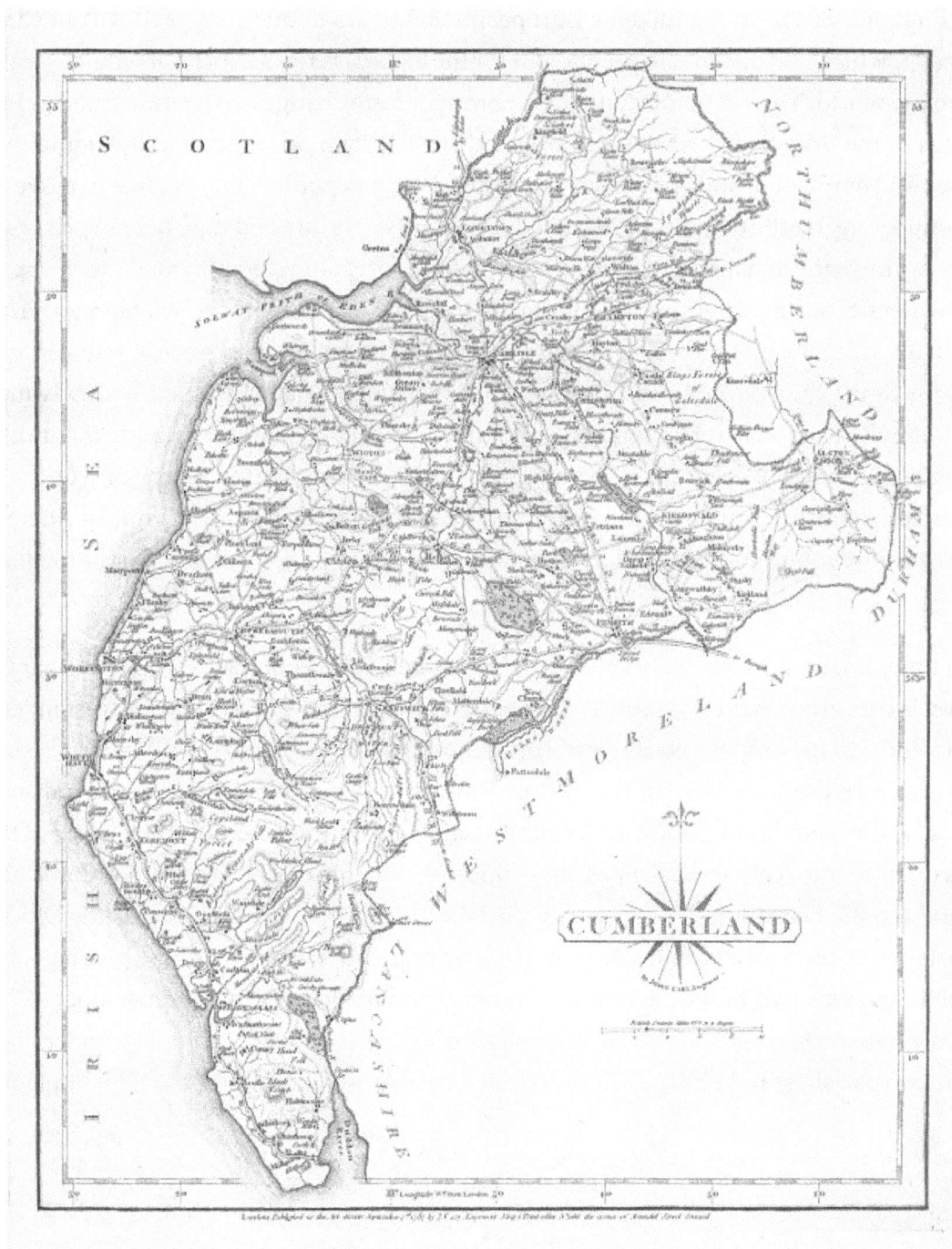

Figure 6 "Cumberland" by John Cary. Copper engraved antique map with original hand colouring published in the 1787 edition of Cary's New and Correct English Atlas.

---

[2] Cumbria Archive Service, Cumbrian Ancestors (Notes for Genealogical Searchers), 2nd ed., September 1993, Cumbria County Council.

In 1974, the county system changed dramatically with the redrawing of boundaries, creation of new counties and the amalgamation of smaller ones. Cumberland was joined with Westmoreland, a part of Lancashire and a part of Yorkshire forming the county of Cumbria as it stands today.

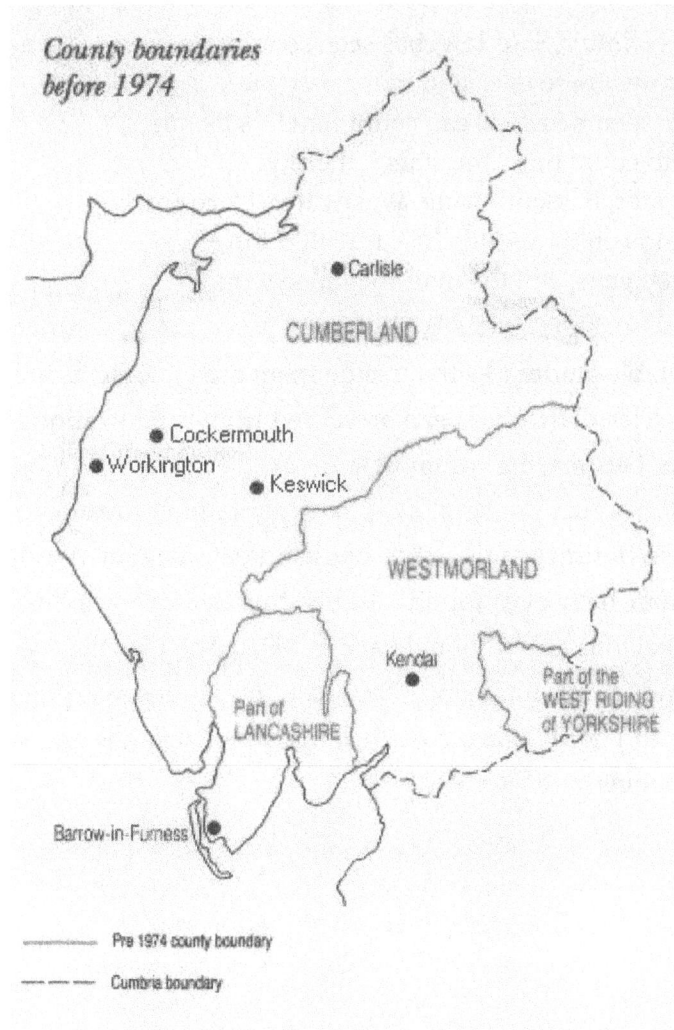

Figure 7 Cumbria County Prior to 1974

The inhabitants and expatriates of Cumberland (Cumbria) have always been fiercely proud of their distinctive landscape, dialect and remoteness from the more prosperous counties in the England to the south. This is no better borne out than in the poem *Canny Cumberland* written by Robert Anderson and published in 1820.

Yer buik-larn'd wise gentry that's seen monie counties,
May preach and palaver, and brag as they will
O' mountains, lakes, valleys, woods, waters, and meadows,
But canny auld Cummerland caps them aw still:
It's true, we've nae palaces sheynin amang us,
Nor marble tall towers to catch the weak eye;
But we've monie feyne cassels, where fit our brave fadders,
When Cummerland cud onie county defy.

Whea that hes climb'd Skiddaw, has seen sec a prospec,
Where fells frown owre fells, and in majesty vie?
Whea that hes seen Keswick, can count hawf its beauties,
May e'en try to count hawf the stars i' the sky:
Theer's Ullswater, Bassenthwaite, Wastwater, Derwent,
That thounsands on thousands ha'e travell'd to view;
The langer they gaze, still the mair they mae wonder,
And ay, as they wonder, may fin summet new.

The poet refers to notable landmarks that reside in an area known as the Lake District in the heart of Cumbria. As a jewel that has been preserved from urbanization and industrialization the Lake District has become the foremost holiday destination in Northern England and fantastic example of Georgian England. Despite exploitation of resources over the centuries, it has retained a sense of timelessness. The English Poet William Wordsworth called it 'the loveliest spot that man hath ever found'. Today this beauty owes its preservation to the declaration of the Lakelands as a National Park in 1951.[3] The Lakelands cover an area of 2,330 square kilometres, and is pre-dominantly farm country dotted with mountains, fells, crags, lakes and waterfalls, all wrapped in a colourful history of struggle and settlement. The story of the Cragg family begins here.

---

[3] The Lake District (A Pitkin Guide), 1994, Pitkin Pictorials Ltd., Great Britain.

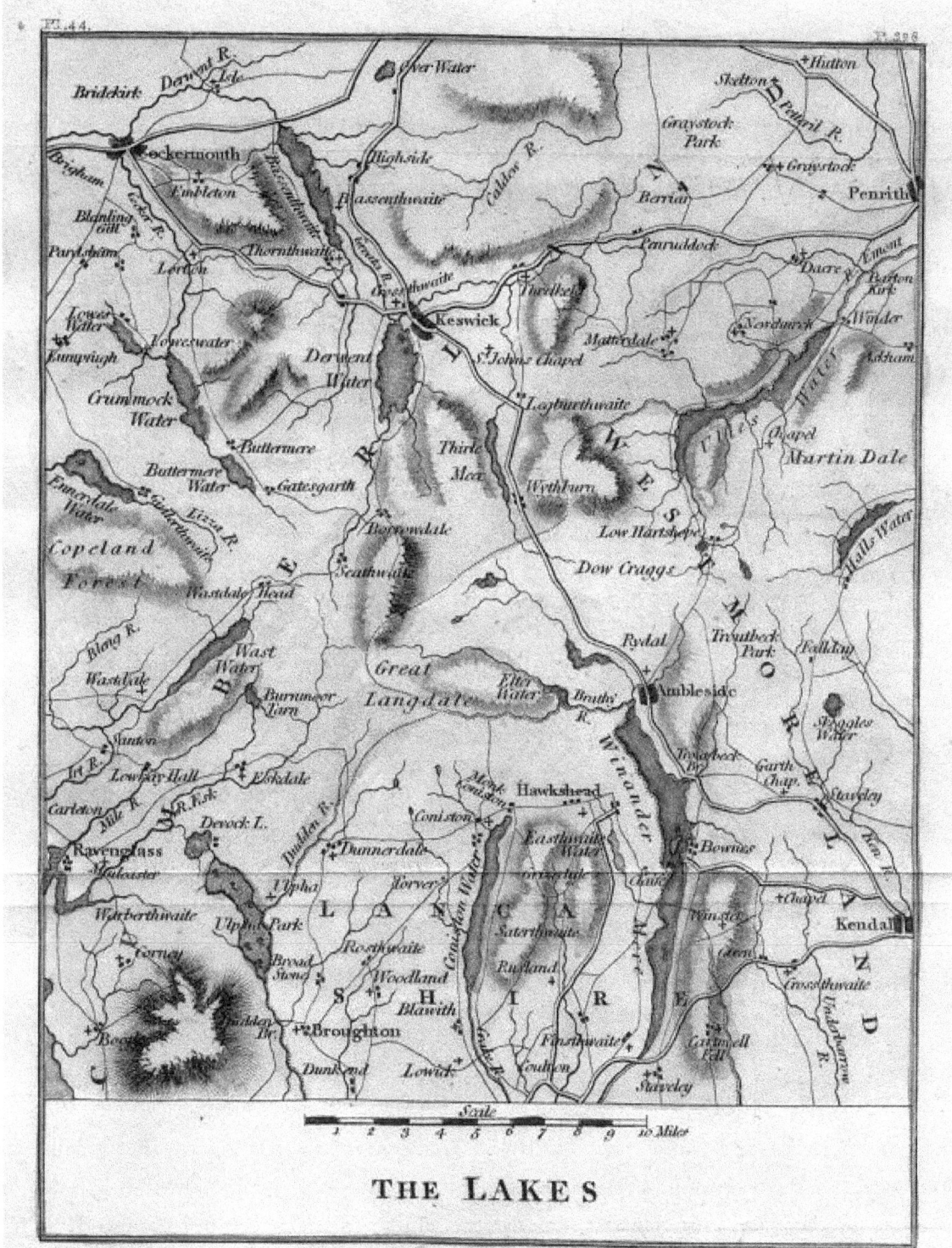

Figure 8 "The Lakes" (Cumberland & Westmoreland) anonymous engraver, published in Guide to all the Watering and Sea Bathing Places ..., about 1810

Chapter Three - Keswick

"Baptism, 1770, September 16th Isaak son of John Cragg and Betty Cragg his wife in the Poorhouse."

Crosthwaite Parish Church Register, Cumberland

The Parish of Crosthwaite in the northern region of England's Lake District, is one of the most beautiful parishes in the area. The principal town is Keswick, in which Crosthwaite Parish Church has existed for hundreds of years on the northern outskirts of the town.

Figure 9 St Kentigern's Church, Great Crosthwaite, Keswick, Cumbria[4]

The name Crosthwaite comes from 'crosfeld'. This derives from a legend that recalls Saint Kentigern placing a cross in a field and preaching to the local people, around 553 AD. Yet others argue that the church itself was established in the 12th century, sparked off by a renewed interest in Saint Kentigern that was taking place at the time. The 'thwaite' in Crosthwaite is actually of Scandinavian origin, and suggests that Vikings also had a hand in

[4] http://www.geog.port.ac.uk/webmap/thelakes/html/lgaz/lk10915.htm, last accessed September 24, 2013

establishing the area and maybe this church. Keswick is understood to mean 'Cheese Farm', and is Anglic in origin.[5]

Figure 10 "Keswick, Derwent &c. from the road to Kendal" engraved by J.Phelps after pictures by Thomas Allom, published in Westmoreland, Cumberland, Durham & Northumberland Illustrated, 1835.

Figure 11 "Keswick, from Greta Bridge" engraved by W.LePetit after pictures by Thomas Allom, published in Westmoreland, Cumberland, Durham & Northumberland Illustrated, 1833.[6]

---

[5] George Bott, Keswick (The Story of a Lake District Town), 1994, Cumbria County Library et. al.

[6] Sourced from http://www.ancestryimages.com/proddetail.php?prod=g7532, last accessed 2 Jan 2016

Keswick, the town, is these days very much a tourist town awash with history and surrounded by majestic natural landscape. On the south-eastern edge of the town is Derwent Water, one the most picturesque lakes in Britain. It runs three miles south, a mile wide, and is host to a few islands that have interesting stories to tell. Beatrix Potter's tale of Squirrel Nutkin is based here, where Nutkin journeys across the lake on a raft in search of nuts. Dominating the town on three sides are the fells Derwent, Castlerigg, and Lonscale. Often these are snow-capped above their slate grey sides, with brown-green lower slopes that line the valleys. The fells themselves have interesting geographical features with names like High Crags, Walla Crags, Black Crag and Cat Bells. It is not difficult to see where inspiration for the Cragg name came from as Cragg and Crag have the same meaning. The most prominent peaks as far as Keswick is concerned are Latrigg and Skiddaw north of Keswick, which loom over the tiny town, leading some commentators to suggest that they add an air of oppression.[7] The remaining area is well farmed with a patchwork quilt of paddocks separated by meandering dry-stone walls. In the mid to late 1700s forests of talk oaks which lined the shores and islands were brought down to service the town and local industries, making way for agricultural land.[8]

Herdwick and Swaledale sheep are the most popular stock. The Swaledale's curious black face peers out at travellers from underneath a substantial thick white fleece, if they happen to disturb its peaceful grazing. Obviously touched by the rural scenes around Keswick, Thomas Sanderson penned this poem in 1820:

> Where Keswick's cliffs o'er hang the dale,
> Responsive to the Shepherd's tale,
> Oft 'midst its wild romantic grots,
> I hear thy long-protracted notes.
> O may no clarions rude invade
> It's peaceful vale, its sylvan shade;
> But, with the rural choir around,
> May thy soft symphonies be found;
> And when I hear the Shepherd's song,
> The bleating flocks that range along,
> The breeze that, though the silent grove,
> Bears the soft sigh that steals from love;
> The Woodman's oft-repeated stroke,
> The stream that falls from the hanging rock,
> The dashing of the neighb'ring mill,
> When all around is dark and still;
> The sweeping oars that gently break

---

[7] James Bunting, The Lake District, 1973, B.T.Bertsford Ltd., London.

[8] John Bowyer Nichols & Sons, The History of the Church of Crosthwaite, Cumberland, 1853.

The slumbers of the peaceful lake,
The music of the vocal lawn,
The Hunter's horn at Morning's-dawn
O! When I hear their chorus swell,
Sweet Echo! give it to thy shell.

The market square is naturally the focal point of activity in Keswick, with its distinctive Moot Hall in the centre, which now houses the Tourist Information Centre. On Market Day, covered stalls are set up in the square and eager sellers draw attention to their goods, with their thick Cumbrian accents bellowing out. This keeps a tradition stretching back to 1276. Some of the more interesting merchandise on sale is the haggis, and Cumberland sausage, which is about a foot long and cooked in a spiral.

Figure 12 Keswick's Market Square (David Cragg 1995)

If you were to stand in the Market Square and wind the clock back to around 1770, Britain and the world stage would be very different from that of today. George III was in his 11th year of reign, while Lord North was Prime Minister of Britain. Captain James Cook claimed Eastern Australia for Britain in April this same year, after he sailed into Botany Bay on the *Endeavour*. In North America, the seeds of revolution were taking root as colonists continually clashed with the British authorities. The most notable confrontation that year was the Boston Massacre where British troops killed five colonists. In 1775, the American Revolution commenced, eventually resulting in Britain losing control of one of its most prized colonies.

Keswick's then cobblestoned market square and main street in 1770 would only have had but a few of the buildings that are still recognisable today. The Moot Hall would be there, but to be rebuilt later in 1812. Main Street was essentially the only street the town really had. Lined with 'timber-framed houses, with enclosures behind for a garden, or an orchard or other domestic use.[9] Beyond these enclosures were open fields. The houses and their yards must have been crowded places as the population in 1787 was around 1,000. The common narrow entrances to the yards were for defensive purposes as the Scots frequently crossed the border to carry out raids from 1138 onwards. With turnpike roads firmly established throughout the country by 1770 the invasions were now of a different kind. It was became fashionable to travel to Keswick, and many notable romantics, writers and commentators made observations, which they subsequently published as tours of enlightenment for their fellow gentry. One such person was Thomas Gray, who visited the area in 1769 and wrote down his romantic observations in his journal 'Tour of the Lakes'. This was later widely read and a source of increased tourism in the area.

> 'In the evening I walked down to the lake... after sunset, and saw the solemn colouring of the night draw on, the last gleam of sunshine fading away on the hilltops, the deep serene of the waters, and long shadows of the mountains.'

Some notable poets consequently flocked to the area, such as Samuel Taylor Coleridge who made his home in Keswick in 1800, living in Greta Hall, and Robert Southey in 1803.[10] The raw unbridled display of nature was a welcome change to the cultivated and high populated south that was steadily embracing the industrial age.

In Newbery and Carnan's *A Description Of England and Wales,* published in 1769, the town of Keswick was unflatteringly described as:

> "greatly decayed, and much inferior to what it was formerly…Keswick has been long noted for having within its neighbourhood mines of the finest black lead in the world; hence it is chiefly inhabited by miners, and many of the poorer inhabitants subsist by carrying on a trade with strolling Jews with black lead clandestinely procured." [11]

---

[9] George Bott, Keswick (The Story of a Lake District Town), 1994, Cumbria County Library et. al.

[10] George Bott, Keswick (The Story of a Lake District Town), 1994, Cumbria County Library et. al.

[11] 1769. Description of England and Wales. : Containing a particular account of each county ... and the lives of the illustrious men each county has produced. Embellished with two hundred and forty copper plates, of palaces, castles, cathedrals; the ruins of Roman and Saxon buildings; and of abbeys, monasteries, and other religious houses. Besides a variety of cuts of urns, inscriptions, and other antiquities, Printed for Newbery and Carman, London

Figure 13 New Map of the Counties of Cumberland and Westmoreland, scale about 4 miles to 1 inch, Emanuel Bowen and Thomas Kitchin, published by T Bowles, John Bowles and Son, Robert Sayer, and John Tinney, 1760[12]

---

[12] http://www.geog.port.ac.uk/webmap/thelakes/html/lgaz/bo18ny21.htm, Last accessed September 24, 2013

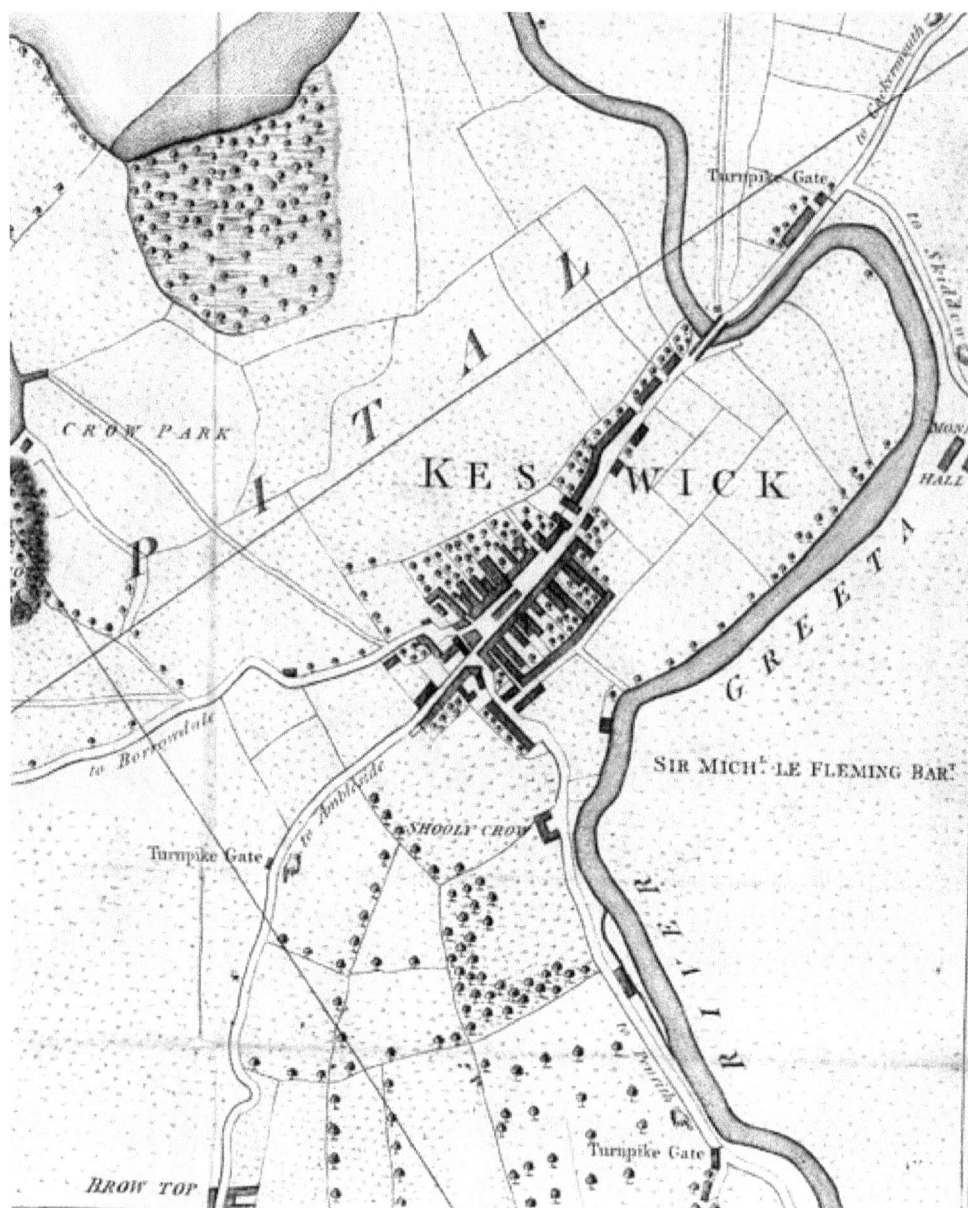

Figure 14 Map series, lakes and roads to the Lakes, by James Clarke, engraved by S J Neele, 352 Strand, London, included in A Survey of the Lakes of Cumberland, Westmorland and Lancashire, published by James Clarke, Penrith, and in London etc., from 1787 to 1793.[13]

Looking again to the Market Square, the weekly markets flourished during this time with trading of the fruit of local industry and agriculture. On sale were salmon, eel, perch, trout, mutton, woollen goods, linen and blankets.[14] A cotton mill had been in operation in the town only a short while on the banks of the Greta, which runs parallel to the main street and empties into the River Derwent. The Industrial Revolution, whilst only thirty years old in 1770 had

[13] http://www.geog.port.ac.uk/webmap/thelakes/html/lgaz/cl152623.htm, last accessed September 24, 2013

[14] George Bott, Keswick (The Story of a Lake District Town), 1994, Cumbria County Library et. al.

already made its presence felt in the Lake District, which will be further evidenced when Cockermouth is discussed later on.

Figure 15 Parish Poor House Keswick Engraving by William Green (Cumbria Images)

Walking northeast along the Market square about 50 metres one would have seen on the right the Parish's 'Poor House', or 'Workhouse'. Betty Cragg resided in the Poor House when she had her son Isaac christened, on 16 September 1770. According to his death certificate, he would have been born in 1766. It is unknown why they were in the Poor House at this time, as the records available do not show them receiving any handouts of money. Thus, we cannot know for sure how long they actually lived in the Poor House either. Poor rates in Keswick in 1770 were 9d in the pound for "the employment of the women and children, spinning, and winding yarn."[15] In England and Wales, under the 1601 Elizabethan Poor Law the poor rate was a tax on property levied on the parish, which provided poor relief to the parish poor.

---

[15] 1770, Arthur Young, A six months tour through the north of England:containing, an account of the present state of agriculture, manufactures and population, in several counties of this kingdom, Printed for W. Strahan

This particular Poor House was built in 1645, during the reign of Charles I, with £200 Sir John Bankes' had bequeathed to raise "a stock of Wool, Flax, Hemp, Thread, Iron and other necessary wear and stuff to set the poor on work who were born in the Parish of Crosthwaite". Every succeeding year £30 from this fund was contributed to what was termed in 1811 as the "manufacture of course [sic] cottons in the town", and was deemed by an observer as being quite a successful endeavour.[16]

Figure 16 Sir John Bankes

The Workhouse held children (who were unable to be kept by their parents), orphans, widows, the ageing poor, and destitute paupers. "Profits from the sale of cloth and linen made by the inmates were to be directed to helping the lame and the blind and the incapacitated, and to organising apprenticeships."[17] The Poor House in Keswick was noted for being more comfortable for the needy than its infamous cousins in larger towns and cities. So much so, it was called the 'Great House', and found itself playing host to up to eighty inmates, amongst them whole families. The Poor Law Amendment Act of 1834 changed this, and made eligibility for entry to the Workhouse more stringent. George Crabbe's description of the typical Poor House in 'The Village'[18] written in 1783 adequately describes the conditions that the inmates of the harsher establishments endured:-

> 'Theirs is yon House that holds the Parish-Poor,
> Whose walls of Mud scarce bear the broken door;
> There, where the putrid vapours, flagging play,
> And the dull wheel hums doleful through the day;-
> There Children dwell who know no Parents' care;
> Parents, who know no Children's love, dwell there!

[16] Worthies (1811 ed.) II. 237. As quoted in C.M.L Bouch and G.P. Jones, The Lake Counties, 1500-1800 by, 1961, Manchester University Press.

[17] George Bott, Keswick (The Story of a Lake District Town), 1994, Cumbria County Library et. al.

[18] George Crabbe, The Village, pp. 16 and 17., 1783

Heart-broken Matrons on the joyless bed,
Forsaken Wives and Mothers never wed;
Dejected Widows with unheeded tears,
And crippled Age with more than childhood fears;
The Lame, the Blind, and, far the happiest they!
The moping Idiot and Madman gay.
Here too the Sick their final doom receive,
Here brought, amid the scenes of grief, to grieve,
Where the loud groans from some sad chamber flow,
Mixt with the clamours of the crowd below;
Here sorrowing, they each kindred sorrow scan,
And the cold charities of man to man:
Whose Laws indeed for ruin'd Age provide,
And strong compulsion plucks the scrap from pride;
But still that scrap is bought with many a sigh,
And pride embitters what it can't deny.'

The Crosthwaite Parish Poor House no longer stands today, as it was torn down and replaced by another building in 1891, which houses Keswick's current Post Office. The only reminder of the Poor house is a plaque on the southern wall of the Post Office that reads:

> "This building stands on the site of the "Workhouse" founded by Sir John Bankes who was born in this town in 1589, became Lord Chief Justice of the Common Pleas and died in Oxford in 1644, his love for his native place and his wise and generous sympathy for the poor and needy, are shewn by the endowment which happily still endures, and is known as 'Sir John Bankes' Charity'."

The baptismal font at Crosthwaite Church at which Isaac was baptised in 1770, dates from King Edward III's time. It was described in 1853.

> The Font stands a little to the north of the west end of the nave, and immediately below the gallery. It is of stone, about four feet high, and has a pyramidal cover of deal, painted to imitate oak. Through efflux of time and much rough usage, it is partially defaced, and further disfigured by applications of lime and white paint. The head or bowl, which is octagonal, rests upon a stem, whose lower portion is of kindred form, though the upper part is quadrangular, and it rises from a sloping surface placed upon a square base. The four faces of the incline have each had a carving of some grotesque figure, now all but obliterated.[19]

---

[19] J.B. Nichols, 1853, The History of the Church of Crosthwaite, Cumberland

Figure 17 Baptismal Font, Crosthwaite Church, Keswick

The Vicar of the church at the time was either Thomas Christian or James Stephen Lushington. Christian died in 1770 after serving the church for 42 years.[20] He was a kinsman of Fletcher Christian of the *Bounty* fame.

There are no concrete clues as what happened to John Cragg after or even while his wife Betty Cragg was pregnant with Isaac. He simply disappears from known records. We can conclude this because it was common for a couple to have a child every two to four years. The next time Betty Cragg brought forth a child is in the following christening entry on 7 September 1783, in the Crosthwaite Parish Register:

> *'Sarah daughter of Betty Cragg, illegitimate'*

That is the last Betty Cragg is heard of, and so it is a mystery as to what happened to the relationship between John and Betty Cragg.

When an illegitimate birth in England occurred during this period, there was sometimes a Bastardry Bond, which the father had to enter as punishment for his lack of moral fibre. It usually meant a guaranteed source of income for the mother and the child.[21] However, in Betty's case no record of such a bond exists at the County Record Office (CRO) in Cumbria.

---

[20] J.B. Nichols, 1853, The History of the Church of Crosthwaite, Cumberland

[21] Cumbria Archive Service, Cumbrian Ancestors (Notes for Genealogical Searchers), 2nd ed., September 1993, Cumbria County Council.

Neither does the CRO have a Settlement Paper or Removal Order for John or Betty Cragg. These documents were used to control the flow of needy people from one Parish to another, and helped prevent Parish resources from becoming over-burdened. The Parish Registers of Great Britain appear to contain no record of a marriage between John and Betty Cragg. However, this is not an uncommon occurrence. There are also no records of a John Cragg being born in Crosthwaite Parish. Thus, his history is very difficult to fathom, especially with a plethora of John Cragg's living in Britain at that time.

In regards to Betty, the following will of Sir Daniel Fleming, 5th Baronet (c.1785–1821) deserves further investigation. It contains valuable last wishes in which he bequeaths as follows:—

> "I give, grant, devise, and bequeath, unto my natural son, Daniel Fleming, of Crosthwaite and Lyth, in the county of Westmorland, viz.—all my lands, both freehold and customary, with the houses and outbuildings, situate in the above-named township, known by the names or commonly called Hill Top, Wincklow, and Calmire Hall, with all belonging to them; likewise, my furniture, plate, books, and live stock, or what else I may then be possessed of at my decease; also my shipping and ropery concerns at Workington and Harrington, the fee farm and penny rents at Crosthwaite, near Keswick, in the county of Cumberland; my said natural son, Daniel Fleming, paying all my just debts and funeral expenses. I leave to Elizabeth Cragg, my housekeeper, the sum of 400l., to be paid a month after my decease. I also leave my child unborn 1,000l., whether boy or girl, to be given it when it arrives at twenty-one, and the interest for maintenance. In case the child should die before it arrives at twenty-one, then the 1,000l. to go to my natural son, Daniel Fleming. I also leave to my brother, Richard Fleming, the sum of 20l.; and to Barbara Benson and Isabella Burrow, each of them 20/., to be paid a month after my decease."[22]

If this were indeed Betty Cragg then she would have been about 70 years of age in 1821. The role of "House Keeper" would be consistent with her son Isaac's occupation in the 1790's, which is discussed in the next section. The residence of Fleming was Rydal Hall, 15 miles south of Keswick.

Another possible lead is the following monumental inscription from a graveyard in the town of Brigham, 3 to 4 km east of Cockermouth.

---

[22] Comprising Reports of Cases in the Courts of Chancery, King's Bench, and Common Pleas, from 1822 to 1835: and Law Journal Reports divided into Equity and Bankruptcy Cases. Common Law Cases 1836-1858, Volume 4, p116.

Erected to the Memory of Samuel Johnston, Woollen Weaver of Cockermouth, who died Nov 15th 1861, Aged 34 years. Also of Elizabeth Cragg his Grandmother who died April 28th 1849 Aged 89 Years.[23]

Whilst John Cragg's burial is not recorded in the Parish Registers of Crosthwaite, this does not necessarily mean he did not die in the Parish. Sometimes the poor were buried without any record of the event. There are some entries of interest in the Gilcrux Parish Bishop's Transcripts (1663-1837). Gilcrux is a small village 20km north-west of Keswick, 8km north of Cockermouth and 5km northeast of Dearham. The entries that interest us are:

1776 'John Cragg (collier, died suddenly) was buried June 27th'

1775 'Joseph son of John Cragg was baptized May 21st'

There are no other Cragg individuals mentioned in the Gilcrux Bishop's Transcripts, which suggests that John Cragg may have relocated here so he could work in one of the local coal mines. The Joseph mentioned in the transcripts may just be Isaac's younger brother. Without additional research, it can only amount to speculation at this stage. The National Burial Index does have the following entry

8 Nov 1825 at Cockermouth John CRAGG aged 74.

Cockermouth was to be the town the Cragg family eventually settled in. If this were the John Cragg we are looking for he would have been about 19 years of age when Isaac was born. Isaac named his first son John in 1795, which suggests that he respected his father and possibly remained in contact with him.

Another possibility is that John Cragg did leave his wife and child to pursue another life or source of employment, and died in another Parish, or perhaps even another country, since the nearest port was just over 20 miles away at Workington. Yet another possibility, albeit fairly slim, could be that John Cragg had joined a British Army Regiment and may have fought in the American War of Independence. The 34th Foot Regiment for example served in North America 1775-1778. This regiment was to be called the 34th (Cumberland) Regiment of Foot. Later, in 1881 it was amalgamated with the 55th (Westmorland) Regiment of Foot (which had also served in North America 1775-1778) to form the Border Regiment. Then in 1959, the Border Regiment joined with the King's Own Royal Regiment (Lancaster) to form the King's Own Royal Border Regiment. This regiment has its Head Quarters at The Castle in Carlisle,

---

[23] Henry Thomas Wake, All the Monumental Inscriptions in the Graveyards of Brigham and Bridekirk, Near Cockermouth In The County of Cumberland 1666 to 1876.

Cumbria.[24],[25] It just may be possible that the records of these regiments can reveal John Cragg's whereabouts after 1770.

Many reasons may have forced Betty Cragg to enter the Poor House. One important source that has not been checked are the Quarter Sessions Records for Cumberland.[26] These may tell us of a conviction brought against John Cragg and a possible sentence, which could explain his absence. Unfortunately, however the real story will likely remain unsolved.

In *Voyage to Sydney in the Ship Hillsborough 1798-1799 and a description of the colony* by William Noah, a John Cragg is mentioned. He had been tried in the Lancaster Quarter Sessions on 17 January 1798, and sentenced to 7 years. The *Hillsborough* sailed from Gravesend, England in October 1798 to Portsmouth. Unfortunately, this John Cragg was 20 years of age at the time of his conviction, and so can be ruled out as a lead.

Also of interest is a biography of a Joseph Birkett published in 1897 as part of the Pennsylvania Biography Project for Lackawanna County in the US[27]:

> The mother of our subject, in maidenhood Ruth Cragg, was born in Cumberlandshire, of Scotch ancestry, and in religious adherence was a Congregationalist, the faith of her family.

This particular Ruth Cragg was the daughter of Isaac Cragg. She had married a John Birkett in 1821. Conceivably the search back into the past may need to venture into Scotland. This could also explain the short-term name change to Craig from Cragg in the late 1800s that a branch of the family undertook in Australia.

---

[24] Richard Simkins, Uniforms of the British Army 1985, Webb and Bower, Great Britain

[25] Arthur Swain (ed.), A Register of the Regiments and Corps of the British Army, 1972, The Archive Press, London.

[26] Cumbria Archive Service, Cumbrian Ancestors (Notes for Genealogical Searchers), 2nd ed., September 1993, Cumbria County Council.

[27] Lackawanna County, Pennsylvania Biography Project – 1897 (PORTRAIT AND BIOGRAPHICAL RECORD. 487 - Joseph Birkett b. 1823)

Chapter Four - Workington

Isaac Cragg of this parish, serving man
Ruth Osburne of this parish, spinster were
married in this church by license this
twenty ninth day of December one thousand
seven hundred and ninety three.
By me Geo: Addison Curate
This marriage was } Isaac X Cragg his mark
solemnized between us } Ruth Osburne X her mark
In the presence of { Joseph Tye & Wm Smith

Marriage No. 50,
Bishops Transcript for 1793 from
St Michaels Church, Workington, Cumberland.

Workington is a seaside industrial town in the county of Cumbria (formerly Cumberland). Barely a 21 mile journey west from Keswick, the town is most well known for the coal field that extends out underneath the Irish Sea. During the 18th and 19th century, the exploitation of the Cumbrian coalfields was extensive. The mining in turn led to the thriving port, from which coal was the chief export.[28]

Figure 18 "Workington" engraved by R.Wallis after a picture by W.H.Bartlett, published in Finden's Ports and Harbours..., 1842

---

[28] John A. Nettleton, Cumbria (Shire County Guide 25), 1989, Shire Publications Ltd.

In 1794, Workington was described in *The History of the County of Cumberland* by William Hutchinson.

This, like most of the small seaport towns, has not been laid out upon a plan of elegance, or for pleasure, but merely for the advantage of those concerned in trade.

From these and other testimonies, it is certain this town cannot boast much importance in antiquity, and that it has arisen from an inferior degree within a century.

The increase of this place has been very rapid of late years, and many of the new buildings are handsome: in the old part of the town the streets are narrow and the houses ill built. The town contains between eleven and twelve hundred houses. The ground-rents for building are lower here than in any part of the county, being no more than One shilling per yard front and twenty backwards.— The river is navigable for ships of four hundred tons burthen. There are now one hundred and sixty vessels belonging to this port, on an average about an hundred and thirty tons each; and every ship of an hundred tons costs 1500*l*. and so in proportion. The chief trade in export is in coals for Ireland, but some few are taken up here for the east country service. The imports, timber, bar-iron, and flax. During the summer season the situation of the place is delightful; but the town cannot boast of many elegant buildings, or the streets of being well paved. The number of inhabitants is computed to exceed six thousand; many are wealthy,, and in general the people are affable and open hearted.

The harbour is esteemed one of the safest upon this coast; the vessels lie secure from the winds of every quarter. Great improvements in the quays have been lately made; much yet remains to be done, to give it all the advantages the situation is so eminently capable of; and, it is to be hoped, for the sake of the public, spirited exertions will not be wanting.—At a bar at the entrance of the harbour the land is sometimes troublesome, but much lessened of late years.

The public manufactories carried on here are of sail-cloth and cordage. An additional ropery is preparing, on a very extended scale. An iron-foundery, which is carried on at a little distance, is mentioned in the sequel.

The public buildings are modern; the church is a handsome structure, with a tower, or steeple, in the Gothic order. The inside of the church is neatly finished, and the altar is ornamented with a painting of our Saviour taken down from the cross. The living, which is one of the best in the county, is in the gift of the Curwen family. About half a mile westward from the town is a spacious workhouse, which, with the easements and out-buildings, cost the inhabitants 1600*l*. and upwards: it is calculated to take in one hundred and fifty persons, though the number now received there does not exceed twenty, including paupers from Harrington, who are taken as boarders. The poor rate is collected by poundage money, at or about the rate of six-pence in the pound. The keeper of the poorhouse is collector of all taxes and assessments, for which he has a yearly salary. — The savings from the poorhouse have amounted in the first year to upwards of two hundred pounds. Too much credit cannot be given to the committee who conduct this business, for their care of the poor, and their attention to the interest of the town.

There is a small but neat assembly-room, which was built at the expense of the present Mr. Curwen; it is well attended during the winter season. Here is also a playhouse, to which Mr. Stordy, who is the head of a company of comedians, gave a handsome subscription. Among the improvements that have taken place within the last twenty years, are the following: — First, A new square in the upper town, consisting of about twenty neat houses. Here the corn market is held. — At no great distance is the butchers' market, where every person has a separate apartment and stall, in the front of which the occupier's name is put up. The bridge leading from the north was erected within the last forty years. The quays have been widened and lengthened considerably, and the bankings increased, within twenty years last past.

Several of those laudable institutions, called Friendly Societies, are held here, one particularly of women, consisting of upwards of two hundred persons: Mrs. Curwen presides as a member, as well as several other very respectable characters.

All workmen of every description, employed under Mr. Curwen, pay to the steward three-pence each every fortnight, at the general payday, as a fund to support the sick, or those who happen misfortunes; to every ten pounds raised by this contribution, Mr. Curwen adds three pounds; the allowance to each sick and disabled man is five shillings a week: as an additional bounty, Mr. Curwen pays their doctor. Here are also the Friendly, Honourable, and Sailors' Societies, the advantages derived from which have been very beneficial.

The markets are in general well supplied, but provisions bear a greater price than in many other parts of Cumberland; shambles meat is seldom under four-pence a pound — salmon from four-pence to two-pence a pound. Cod is plentiful, some years selling at a halfpenny a pound. Herrings are brought from the Isle of Man, and frequently from Whitehaven, when that market is overstocked.

The coal trade is of the greatest importance. There are two sets of workings almost contiguous to Workington; nine pits, belong to Mr. Curwen, and five to Mr. Walker, as agent to the trustees of Anthony Bacon, Esq. M. P. London; they generally ship, on account of both parties, about an hundred and fifty wagon loads per day, (Sunday excepted).

The collieries here have their obstructions, or troubles, as the miners call them, equally with those at Whitehaven, and other places on this coast. The pits are from forty to ninety fathoms in depth, having generally two or three workable bands. Mr. Curwen is at this time employed is endeavouring to open the Chapel-bank colliery: the shaft now sinking is upwards of twelve feet diameter. There are two fire-engines upon it; the pumpingengine one of the most powerful ever erected in Cumberland. Should this work be crowned with success, the advantage to the town cannot fail of being very great, both from the quality and extent of the coal: that heretofore worked has been nothing but the out-burst.

In the coal-works are between five and fix hundred persons employed. The fireengines have greatly lessened the number of horses used, which is a matter of much advantage both to the public and the proprietor; and, we may venture to say, in a very few years fire-engines alone will be used in the drawing up of coals. An engine sufficient to draw coals from ninety fathoms may be erected for 600*l*.:— more than half that sum would in the first instance be required to purchase horses necessary for the drawing up of coal.

The road from the collieries to the haven belongs to Mr. Curwen, and he receives a yearly payment from Mr. Walker for his accommodation. The coal in general is of a good quality, and is sold to the inhabitants at the rate of two shillings for a single horse cart load, containing four customary bushels: the kennal coals for one shilling and four-pence, of the like measure. Mr. Curwen's pits being most contiguous, supply the inhabitants chiefly.

Lord Lonsdale's estate adjoins upon the estate of Mr. Curwen, on the north and cast of Workington.

The manor-house of the family of Curwens, called Workington-hall, stands upon a fine eminence on the banks of the river Derwent. It is an elegant mansion, surrounded with excellent lands: the house commands a prospect of the town, the river and its northern banks, and the western ocean for a considerable tract. Here is a park, with beautiful cattle.[29]

St. Michaels Church, which overlooks the town, has stood for over three hundred years. Tragically gutted in late 1994, in a fire started by vandals. Fortunately, the stonework survived, and the church has since been restored to its former glory. The church, previously rebuilt in 1770 was described in 1847:

"It consists of nave, with a low square tower, which formed part of the old fabric, and is lighted by two rows of round headed windows. Over a recess, which contains the altar table, is window of three lights, with the top filled stained glass; on the north side is a painting of Christ taking down from the Cross, and on the South another representing the Ascension. The effigies of a knight and his lady recline on an altar-tomb under the tower, near to which is part of an ancient octagonal stone font..."[30]

---

[29] Hutchinson , William. 1794 *The History of the County of Cumberland*

[30] Directory of Cumberland, 1847

Figure 19 St Michaels Church, Workington

St Michaels is in the Diocese of Chester, Archdeaconry of Richmond, Deanery of Copeland, and the Parish of St. Michaels. It is important to note that its marriage bonds and allegations up until 1854 are held in the archives of Lancashire County.

Isaac Cragg sometime between 1770 and 1793 came to live in Workington Parish where he met his future wife. If he was still living with his mother when his half-sister Sarah was born in 1783, he may have arrived in Workington sometime after that date. Unfortunately, this cannot presently be verified. As a serving man, he may have lived at the residence where he worked, or in very modest accommodation nearby. Servants were generally hired for a year at a time at one of the periodic hiring fairs held around Whitsuntide (seventh Sunday after Easter) and Martinmas (11 November). In between the terms of service servants enjoyed a week's holiday, which was usually, spent visiting relatives. From the church register entry, we know he was unable to write legibly, as he used a mark, usually in the form of a cross, to indicate his signature to the marriage. This also reveals he did not receive reasonable education, which is common for this period, as children were usually sent off to work as young as possible.

The register entry also mentions the couple were married by license. In Isaac and Ruth's day, the Church of England recognised two formal procedures, one of which was to be followed before marriage took place. The first was a "calling of the banns", which was a public declaration of their intention to marry. The second more private method was to obtain a marriage license, that they would in turn present to the priest who was to marry them. In this case, it would have been the curate George Addison.[31] Not many licenses exist because many priests simply kept them instead of passing them onto the Diocese of Chester's Registry. However, the sworn statement (allegation) made by the couple to a diocesan official (so they could be issued with a license) still exists in the Lancashire Record Office. This statement holds information such as names, ages, marital conditions, residence and occupations of Ruth and Isaac.[32] The marriage bond and allegation tell us that Isaac and Ruth were 21 and 26 years of age respectively. Isaac's witness for the bond was a male with the surname McIntosh, a farmer of the parish. If the bond were to be broken, Isaac would owe the Lord Bishop of Chester £200. Isaac signed the bond with an awkward vertical pen stroke between his first name and surname. Following his surname is a wax seal. This could be Isaac's personal seal, which served as a signature in those days, or an official confirmation that he indeed was the person who signed it. Unfortunately, it is impossible to make out any detail in the copy we have. The allegation states that Ruth lived in Winscales in the four weeks leading up to the wedding. Winscales, within the Parish of Workington, is a village three miles southeast of Workington's town centre.

Ruth was originally from the Parish of Holme Cultram, some 15-20 miles north of Workington. She was christened in Holme Cultram 11 May 1771. Her father was Solomon Osburn and mother Ruth Messenger, whom he had married 24 October 1763 in Holme

---

[31] Cumbria Archive Service, Cumbrian Ancestors (Notes for Genealogical Searchers), 2nd ed., September 1993, Cumbria County Council.

[32] Cumbria Archive Service, Cumbrian Ancestors (Notes for Genealogical Searchers), 2nd ed., September 1993, Cumbria County Council.

Cultram. The Messenger name goes back centuries in Cumberland's history. The main focal point for generations of the Messenger family was the town of Maryport, where they were well established in trade.[33] Solomon surprisingly lived to be 102 years old, dying in 1839. The following death notice appeared in the *Carlisle Journal* on April 20 that year.

> At Cow Gate, in the parish of Holm Cultram, lately, Solomon OSBORNE, yeoman, in his 103rd year. This old patriarch retained all his faculties, with the exception of sight, to the very last. He never could be brought to believe in the power of steam; when taken to the beach by his friends to see the steamers pass and repass, he still persisted that they were impelled by the wind.[34]

The *Gentleman' Magazine* in 1839 published the following tribute:

> At Holme Cultram, Mr. Solomon Osborne, in his 106th year. He retained his faculties in a remarkable degree to his latest hour, and had a lively recollection of the gathering of the population armed with pitchforks, &c. marching to oppose the rebels at Carlisle, in 1745.[35]

The rebels referred to was the Jacobite rising of 1745, often referred to as "The 'Forty-Five", which was the attempt by Charles Edward Stuart "Bonnie Prince Charlie" to regain the British throne for the exiled House of Stuart, and recreate an absolute monarchy in the Kingdom of Great Britain. On 8 November 1745, Charles, with an escort of Lochiel's Camerons and the hussars, entered England. On 9 November, the hussars sent a captured countryman to Carlisle, requesting that it provide quarters for 13,000 infantry and 3,000 cavalry or otherwise the city would be burnt. A string of cannon shots came from the city walls and the hussars retreated. Jacobite forces then besieged Carlisle until it surrendered two days later on the 15th. The surrender conditions were that the defenders of Carlisle must agree not to fight against Jacobite forces for one year and that the militia must give up their arms. On 16 November, the mayor of Carlisle delivered the keys of the city to Charles at Brampton. Charles entered Carlisle that same day riding a white charger accompanied by 100 bagpipers, with cheering Highlanders lining the streets. Salutes of cannon and muskets accompanied the constant ringing of church bells. The Jacobites extorted 1,500 muskets, 160 barrels of gunpowder, 500 grenades and about 120 horses from the city. The Duke of Cumberland believed that "the surrender of Carlisle to the rebels was the source of all the distress this part of the kingdom has felt from them and it of so scandalous a nature that it deserves the strictest enquiry and punishment". The Jacobites eventually lost control of Carlisle in a siege, lasting from 21 December to the 30th.

---

[33] David Hey, The Oxford Guide to Family History, 1993, Oxford University Press.

[34] Carlisle Journal, Saturday 20 Apr 1839 (p. 3, col. 6-7)

[35] "DEATHS", 1839, The Gentleman's Magazine: and historical review, July 1856-May 1868, , pp. 441-447.

The *West Cumberland Times* also recorded Solomon Osborne's remarkable age in 1892. When Isaac and Ruth were married, Ruth was already three months pregnant, though this was not such a scandal in those days as ten percent of marriages took place after the birth of the first child. Thus, the expected baby probably encouraged the couple to get married. Sometime in the next six months between January and June of 1794, the newly wedded Isaac and Ruth moved to the town of Cockermouth. This was to be the hometown of the Cragg family for many years to come.

Chapter Five - Cockermouth

Figure 20 Cockermouth: engraved by R.Sands after a picture by Thomas Allom, published in *Westmoreland,*
Cumberland, Durham & Northumberland Illustrated, **1832.**

In 1794, George III was in his 35th year as King. William Pitt, in his 11th year in office, was the youngest Prime Minister Britain had ever seen. Across the Channel, the French Revolutionary War had begun the previous year. With the threat posed by French Armies invading the Austrian Netherlands, Britain was drawn into halting the French advance. On 1 February 1793, France declared war on Britain, which was to stretch out into 23 years of intermittent conflict eventually culminating in the Napoleon's defeat at Waterloo. The most notable military engagement of 1794 was the British naval victory over the French called the Glorious First of June.[36]

---

[36] J. P. Kenyon, The Wordsworth Dictionary of British History, 1994, Wordsworth Editions Ltd., Hertfordshire, England.

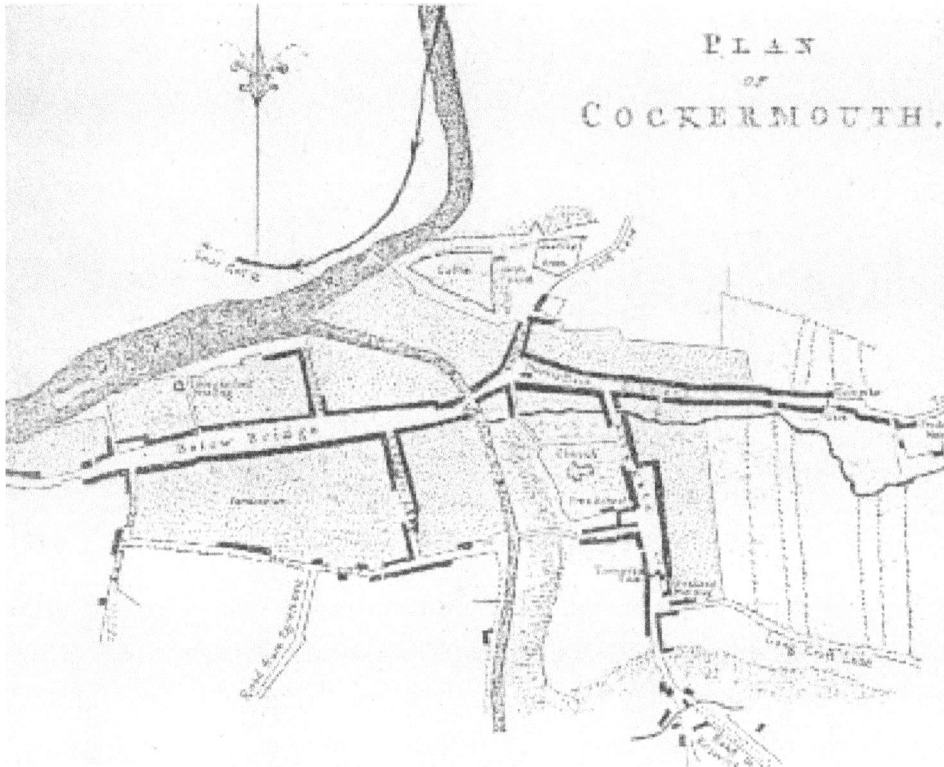

Figure 21 Map of Cockermouth 1775 by Hodkinson and Donald

Isaac and Ruth Cragg moved to the market town of Cockermouth in early 1794, having travelled seven miles east, going back towards Keswick, which was thirteen miles before Cockermouth.

> "Cockermouth is a borough and market town, in the Parish of Brigham, and in the ward of Allerdale above Derwent, 305 miles from London, 25 from Carlisle, 15 from Whitehaven, and 7 from Maryport and Workington. It is seated on the south side of the river Derwent, and is at the mouth of the Cocker, whence its name is derived; the latter river flowing through the town previous to its junction with the Derwent is crossed by a bridge connecting the eastern and south-western parts of the town. Another bridge of two arches, 270 feet in length, crosses the Derwent. The town, although neat and clean, is not regularly built; lying between two hills, upon one of which are the remains of an ancient castle, and upon the other, the Church of All Saints" [37]

---

[37] Pigots 1830 Directory.

Figure 22 Cockermouth Castle 1816

Situated so close to Scotland, Cumberland endured a turbulent history known as the "Border troubles". In 1069 Malcolm, King of Scotland had sided with the discontented Saxons against William the Conqueror, who finally subdued both parties, bringing the town of Cockermouth under England's control. William's son, Henry I, gifted Cumberland to Randolph de Mechines (now pronounced Messenger), in recognition of his services to his father during the conquest. It is interesting to note that the maiden name of Ruth's mother was Messenger.[38] Randolph's younger brother William was made Baron of Egremont.[39] It is widely believed that the Castle at Cockermouth was first built by William or the Earl of Dunbar in 1134, mainly from stone retrieved from a former Roman settlement, in what is now called Papcastle.

> This barony was given by William de Meschines to Waldeof, son of Gospatric, Earl of Dunbar, whose grand-daughter brought it to William Fitz-Duncan, nephew of Malcolm, King of Scotland; one of the co-heiresses of Fitz-Duncan, who was twice married, died without issue; the two others, whose issue eventually shared this barony in moieties, married William Le Gros, Earl of Albemarle, and Reginald De Lucy; the heiress of Lucy married Multon, who took the name of Lucy. After the death of William de Fortibus, Earl of Albemarle, and Isabel his countess, without issue, a moiety of the castle and honor of Cockermouth fell to the crown, and having been for a while in the possession of Piers Gaveston, by the grant of Edward II was some years afterwards, (1323), granted to Anthony Lord Lucy already possessed by inheritance of the other moiety. Maud, sister and heiress of Anthony Lord Lucy, who died in 1366, settled the castle and honor of Cockermouth on Henry Percy, Earl of Northumberland, her second husband, and his heirs male, on condition that they should bear the arms of Lucy quarterly with their own. Elizabeth, sole heiress of Josceline, the last Earl of Northumberland, brought Cockermouth and other large estates to Charles Seymour, Duke of Somerset. Lady Catherine, second daughter and coheiress of the duke,

---

[38] *Askew, John. 1866 A guide to the interesting places in and around Cockermouth*

[39] Hutchinson , William. 1794 *The History of the County of Cumberland*

married Sir William Wyndham, whose son Sir Charles, was in 1749 created Earl of Egremont, and was father of George Earl of Egremont, the present possessor of the honor or barony of Cockermouth.[40]

In late 1297, William Wallace, together with a large band of Scots raided England and soon pillaged Northumberland and Cumberland. Carlisle Castle withstood a short siege, before Wallace and his men marched away on 8 December, 'devastating everything, by way of the forest of Inglewood, Cumberland and Allerdale to the Derwent at Cockermouth'.[41] On their return to Scotland via Northumberland, they again left a trail of destruction, putting 700 villages to the torch. [42]

King Robert Bruce and the Black Douglas invaded Cumberland in 1315 and laid waste the whole district from Cockermouth to St. Bees, plundering the Monastery of St. Bees, destroying the manor houses of Cleator and Stainburn, and pillaging the church at Brigham. It has also been suggested he damaged the castle at Cockermouth. For three days in 1387, the Earl of Fife, with the Earl of Douglas and the Lord of Galloway, led an army of thirty thousand Scots on a campaign in which the area suffered greatly. They attempted to take the castle by surprise, but were unsuccessful. [43]

Mary Queen of Scots took refuge in Cockermouth Hall one night in May 1568 under the care of Henry Fletcher following the defeat of her forces in 1568 in the Battle of Langside. During her stay, Henry presented her with crimson velvet fabric from which to make a new robe, after having observed the poor condition of her clothing. The family was later knighted for this kindness, by her son James I. The following morning she left with her party to journey to Carlisle and eventual imprisonment. Mary was later beheaded on 8 February 1587 (aged 44) at Fotheringhay Castle, Northamptonshire.

The Castle at Cockermouth later featured in the English Civil War.

> In the year 1648 it was garrisoned by King Charles I., and was soon after laid siege to by the Parliamentary forces under General Cromwell, who raised a fort against it, distant to the south-west about a quarter of a mile, above Fitz House. The way to this fort, which is still in a good state of preservation, is by Sullart Street. The side of the fort commanding the castle is a half-moon battery, the inner ditch being still eight or

[40] 'Cockermouth', Magna Britannia: volume 4: Cumberland (1816), pp. 40-45. URL: http://www.british-history.ac.uk/report.aspx?compid=50681 Date accessed: 27 August 2013.
[41] Rothwell, Henry: *The Chronicle of Walter of Guisborough, p. 305*
[42] Askew, John. 1866 *A guide to the interesting places in and around Cockermouth*
[43] Askew, John. 1866 *A guide to the interesting places in and around Cockermouth*

nine feet deep. Here Cromwell and his Ironsides lighted their watch fires, dug their trenches, devoutly reading their Bibles, singing psalms and hymns, as each relieved other in their labours. A strong body of troops held the town. All the chief approaches from the country were vigilantly guarded. Outlying picquets, and small bodies of well-mounted cavalry, held possession of all the surrounding villages. They were God-fearing men,—many of them preachers. Those who kept guard over the villages of Great and Little Broughton, were the founders of a church of Baptists, which ultimately developed into an important body of religionists. "In that singular camp" says Lord Macaulay, "no oath was heard, no drunkenness or gambling was seen; the property of the peaceable citizens, and the honour of women were held sacred. No servant-girl complained of the rough gallantry of the red coats. Every thing they purchased was paid for to, the full value. Not one ounce of plate was taken from the shops of the jewellers or" goldsmiths." A few days sufficed to complete the fort. The field guns were unlimbered, placed in position, and after a short but well directed cannonade, the south-west wall was breached. Cromwell and his Ironsides marched to the assault, sword in hand, carrying all before them. The castle was taken, and the garrison made prisoners of war. Cromwell repaired the walls he had blown down, and left a small force to hold the place in possession for the Parliament. This garrison was in turn besieged, for one month, by a party of Cumberland Royalists, but without success. Lieutenant Brier, the governor, held out till Colonel Ashton (whom Cromwell sent from Lancashire) arrived, who attacked and dispersed the besiegers. During the siege, twelve of the Royalists were killed; and we find their names duly inserted in the burial register of All Saints', for the month of September, 1648.

When all the Royalists in the neighbourhood were finally subdued, the Parliamentary soldiers, before evacuating the place, dismantled and set fire to the greater part of it. The gateway arid flagstaff-tower they left uninjured, and in these the Quarter Sessions for the County were held for many years. The ruined parts were carted away by the inhabitants in great quantities for some time, many houses in the town being built from the materials thus obtained.[44]

The town has seen many other famous faces in its streets such as James I and Robert Louis Stevenson. Two notable people born in the town were the poet William Wordsworth and The Bounty mutineer Fletcher Christian. Wordsworth was born on 7 April 1770, in a large Georgian house that still stands in Main Street. He went on to be perhaps England's most famous poet, earning the title Poet Laureate in 1842. His poem, 'The Prelude', recalls memories of the time spent in Cockermouth until 1778; in particular the river Derwent that flowed behind his house.[45]

---

[44] *Askew, John. 1866 A guide to the interesting places in and around Cockermouth*

[45] *The Works of William Wordsworth*, 1994, The Wordsworth Poetry Library, Wordsworth Editions Ltd., Hertfordshire, England.

Was it for this
That one, the fairest of all rivers, loved
To blend his murmurs with my nurse's song,
And, from his alder shades and rocky falls,
And from his fords and shallows, sent a voice
That flowed along my dreams? For this, didst thou
O Derwent! winding among grassy holms
Where I was looking on, a babe in arms,
Make ceaseless music that composed my thoughts
to more than infant softness, giving me
Amid the fretful dwellings of mankind
A foretaste, a dim earnest, of the calm
That nature breathes among the hills and groves.
When, having left his Mountains, to the Towers
Of Cockermouth that beauteous River came,
Behind my Father's House he pass'd, close by,
Along the margin of our Terrace Walk.
He was a Playmate whom we dearly lov'd.
Oh! many a time have I, a five years' Child,
A naked Boy, in one delightful Rill,
A little Mill-race sever'd from his stream,
Made one long bathing of a summer's day,
Bask'd in the sun, and plunged, and bask'd again
Alternate all a summer's day, or cours'd
Over the sandy fields, leaping through groves
Of yellow grunsel, or when crag and hill,
The woods, and distant Skiddaw's lofty height,

William Hutchinson published a description of Cockermouth in 1794, the same year Isaac and Ruth arrived. Together with *The Universal British Directory of Trade, Commerce, and Manufacture Vol. 2*, which was published between 1790-98 a reasonable picture of 1790s Cockermouth can be constructed. Hutchinson in some cases appears to have directly quoted the directory for some of his comments.

The eye, after having run over a variety of pleasing objects, now viewed this ancient town with no small degree of delight. The castle appeared on our approach, crowning an eminence on the left, the church on the right, between which lay the road into the town. On our first entrance, the town-house, with the adjoining buildings, prejudiced us with an immediate idea that here we would find no other than the marks of decayed grandeur: but we were agreeably disappointed.[46]

Cockermouth is a chapelry in the parish of Brigham. It stands at the mouth of the river Cocker, from whence the name is derived. The town lies upon both banks of the river, with a communication by a bridge. The river Derwent washes the western foot of the eminence on which the castle is built, and at its southern point receives the Cocker. [47] The river divides the town into two parts nearly equal; the church, market-place, and castle, standing on the East fide, and the other part on the-South-west.[48]

The town is irregular, yet has many modern and well-built houses.[49] The houses form two streets, in an angular figure, from the bend of which runs out the short street that leads to the castle.[50] The street ascending to the castle-gate is particular, though from the steepness of the hill not so commodious a situation as the others in the town, yet seems to be the favourite of people of fortune, and contains many genteel buildings. A spacious street leads to Derwent-bridge: some of the houses are of red tree-stone, and make a handsome appearance.[51] One of these chief streets stands above the river Cocker, in which are the moot-hall, market-house, and shambles, which have a gloomy and antique appearance. These erections are in general great obstacles and disagreeable objects in our northern towns: they are without exception dirty and unwholesome. These at Cockermouth are not so great a nuisance as others we have seen, but yet are disgusting, and an annoyance as well to the passenger as inhabitant. On the other side Cocker the corn market is held. The street on the other side of that river runs parallel with the Derwent; is spacious, open, and well built; and here the market for cattle is held. [52]

The castle stands on the conflux of the rivers Derwent and Cocker, upon an eminence which commands an extensive and beautiful prospect. The Castle, [is] now in ruins, except some apartments at the gate.[53] Its ruins are much admired by travellers, and it is supposed to be of ancient structure. The whole fortress forms an irregular square: in former ages this was a place of great extent and strength. 54 On the gates are the arms

---

[46] Hutchinson , William. 1794 *The History of the County of Cumberland*

[47] Hutchinson , William. 1794 *The History of the County of Cumberland*

[48] *The Universal British Directory of Trade, Commerce, and Manufacture Vol. 2. 1790-98*

[49] *The Universal British Directory of Trade, Commerce, and Manufacture Vol. 2. 1790-98*

[50] Hutchinson , William. 1794 *The History of the County of Cumberland*

[51] *The Universal British Directory of Trade, Commerce, and Manufacture Vol. 2. 1790-98*

[52] Hutchinson , William. 1794 *The History of the County of Cumberland*

[53] Hutchinson , William. 1794 *The History of the County of Cumberland*

[54] Hutchinson , William. 1794 *The History of the County of Cumberland*

of the Multons, Umfranvilles, Lucys, and Percys, but they are now partly defaced. The approach has been kept by a draw-bridge over a deep ditch. The gateway appears to be more modern than any other part of the building, is vaulted with ribbed arches joining in the centre, and defended with a portcullis, over which is a lofty tower. Authors differ about the founder of this castle, though they agree that it was built soon after the conquest.[55] In the year 1648, this castle being garrisoned for the king, was reduced by the parliamentary forces, burnt, or otherwise dismantled; and has lain totally in ruins.[56]

This is a very ancient borough, and sent members to parliament in the 23rd year of the reign of King Edward I. It discontinued this franchise for several centuries. The first regular returns we find in modern times proceed from the year 1640. The election is by inhabitants having burgage tenure, who are about three hundred in number; and the bailiff of the borough is returning officer. He is chosen yearly at Michaelmas out of the burghers, by the jury of the Leet, which is composed of burghers, and forms a special jury [of sixteen burgesses] [57] for the government of the borough, at the court then held for the borough: and, being head officer within the town, he executes the duty of clerk of the marker, which, by custom, is annexed to his bailiwick. [58]

The borough now sends two members to parliament. They are chosen by the inhabitants at large; but the right hon. the Earl of Lonsdale, being now in possession of the majority of the borough-votes, having purchased the greatest part of the houses in the borough at a most enormous price, is careful that they are tenanted by such only as will obey his recommendation as implicitly as the fourteen hundred colliers he caused to be made in one day freemen of Carlisle. His lordship, exclusive of his property in the town, is lord of part of the manor. The right hon. the Earl of Egremont has also a very great property here, the castle and lands belonging to it being his. He is also lord of the manor of part of Cockermouth by descent from William de Meschines. [59]

The advantages which Cockermouth has over the neighbouring towns are many, being an excellent situation for trade and manufactories, the surrounding Country populous and fertile, having a constant and plentiful supply of water by different streams, several valuable coal-mines, and three sea-ports, all within the small distance

[55] *The Universal British Directory of Trade, Commerce, and Manufacture Vol. 2. 1790-98*

[56] Hutchinson , William. 1794 *The History of the County of Cumberland*

[57] *The Universal British Directory of Trade, Commerce, and Manufacture Vol. 2. 1790-98*

[58] Hutchinson , William. 1794 *The History of the County of Cumberland*

[59] *The Universal British Directory of Trade, Commerce, and Manufacture Vol. 2. 1790-98*

of 15 miles. The turnpike-roads are also in very good order. [60] There are four bridges, which are supported by the public. Derwent [Gote] bridge, Cocker bridge, Isel bridge and Ouse bridge. [61]

The market is held on Monday weekly is well supplied with provisions and grain. Every fortnight there are shews of horned cattle on the Wednesdays in the great street, from the beginning of May till Michaelmas [10th October] where is shewn a great number of good horses, this being the only annual horse-fair held in Cockermouth.[62] There are likewise two general fairs held in the market-place, on Whitsun Monday and Martinmas Monday, for hiring servants. [63] On the hiring-day the fair is held in the Castle-yard, the cattle-fair in the spacious street below the bridge, and the horse-fair on the common adjoining called Gallow-barrow. [64]

The principal articles manufactured in this place are tanned leather, the annual profits on which amount to about 14,000l. hats, mostly for exportation, the annual returns on which are about 7,000l. and shalloons and other coarse woollens, on which the annual returns are about 6,000l.. There is also a manufactory for coarse linen cloth. [65]

Men's wages on an average 10l. a year, and women's wages 4l a year.—There is a considerable manufactory carried on of hats, which employs about one hundred hands;—of coarse woollen cloths and shalloons[66], in which about three hundred hands are employed ;— of checks and coarse linens, with about fifty hands;—and the leather trade, in various branches, employs about fifty hands. The whole place bears the countenance of opulence. [67]

In the year 1785, an accurate calculation was made of the people of the town of Cockermouth, when we found that there were 663 families, and 2652 inhabitants.[68] It is remarkable, that the average number of persons to a family was no more than four. Since that time there has been no material change in the population of this place. [69]

---

[60] *The Universal British Directory of Trade, Commerce, and Manufacture Vol. 2. 1790-98*

[61] Hutchinson , William. 1794 *The History of the County of Cumberland*

[62] *The Universal British Directory of Trade, Commerce, and Manufacture Vol. 2. 1790-98*

[63] Hutchinson , William. 1794 *The History of the County of Cumberland*

[64] *The Universal British Directory of Trade, Commerce, and Manufacture Vol. 2. 1790-98*

[65] *The Universal British Directory of Trade, Commerce, and Manufacture Vol. 2. 1790-98*

[66] Shalloons - A lightweight wool or worsted twill fabric, used chiefly for coat linings or a band for tying the tail of a wig, made of such material.

[67] Hutchinson , William. 1794 *The History of the County of Cumberland*

[68] Hutchinson , William. 1794 *The History of the County of Cumberland*

[69] Hutchinson , William. 1794 *The History of the County of Cumberland*

The church, dedicated to All-Saints, first built in the reign of Edward III was rebuilt in 1711.[70] It was entirely rebuilt from the ground, all but the tower and rendered very commodious for the large congregation, which resorts to it: it is one hundred feet in length, and forty-five broad, and lined with galleries. The income of the curacy was certified at 34l. 13s. 4d. Lord Lonsdale being impropriator, nominates the curate. Lord Lonsdale has both the great and small tithes, said to be worth about 100l. a year, out of which he pays the curate's stipend of 26l. 13s. 4d. and 10l. per annum to the master of the free-school. [71]

Robert Rickarby, who was incumbent before the civil war, was suspended during the usurpation by George Larkham, an independent; at the restoration, Rickarby recovered his church, died in February, 1699, and was buried in Cockermouth. He was succeeded by Thomas Jefferson, A. M. of Queen's College, Oxford, who died in February, 1768, and was buried at Cockermouth. Since that time no one has been nominated to this church. However Vicar Joseph Gilbanks from Kirkland Parish is listed as Clergy under the title of lecturer. It is remarkable, that there have been only two incumbents since the year 1640. This chapel has never received augmentation. [72]

The church is built of freestone, the ancient tower remaining; a set of six bells, with a clock and chime: no aisles. The altar-piece is ornamented with paintings of Moses and Aaron. There is a parochial library kept in a room over the freeschool.[73]

There is one dissenting and one Quaker meeting-house here; the families of dissenters about 120 in number—the Quaker families about 30. [74]

The free grammar school was founded soon after the reformation, and now contains about 30 scholars.—A charity school, instituted in 1784, and supported by a voluntary subscription of 21l. per annum, now contains 63 scholars; a Sunday school instituted in 1785, and supported by the offerings at the monthly communions, receives near 100 scholars; besides these there are several private schools, which receive upon an average about 25 scholars each. [75]

---

[70] *The Universal British Directory of Trade, Commerce, and Manufacture Vol. 2. 1790-98*

[71] Hutchinson , William. 1794 *The History of the County of Cumberland*

[72] Hutchinson , William. 1794 *The History of the County of Cumberland*

[73] Hutchinson , William. 1794 *The History of the County of Cumberland*

[74] Hutchinson , William. 1794 *The History of the County of Cumberland*

[75] Hutchinson , William. 1794 *The History of the County of Cumberland*

There is very little freehold land in Cockermouth, but many of the inhabitants have freehold estates in other manors. [76] The annual value of lands and houses somewhat exceeds 4000l. a year: the poor rates annually amount to about 1s. 6d. in the pound; in the workhouse there are about forty paupers; but several out-pensioners are added to that number.—There are four friendly societies, confiding of nearly five hundred members. These societies hold out an example to the rest of the kingdom; for, besides the comfortable relief they afford to their sick and reduced brethren, in Cockermouth they have relieved the poor rate so much, that, about ten years ago, the annual collection amounted to 4s. in the pound. [77]

There was a spacious park for deer appertaining to the baronial mansion here, extending from the town eastward about a mile; but being disparked, the lands have been brought into cultivation. [78]

A school was founded in the town of Cockermouth by Philip Lord Wharton, Sir George Fletcher, Sir Richard Graham, and others; the endowment produces 26l. a year and upwards, arising from various payments[79]

The situation of Cockermouth is low and warm, sometimes fogs in the evenings, yet very healthy, as appears by the register, as not above one person in forty dies annually. It is well watered, for, besides the two greater rivers, there are also two rivulets, which afford great accommodation to the manufacturers. The rivers abound with salmon, trout, brandling, pike, eels, and other smaller fish. [80] Beneath the Derwent is a plain of considerable extent, in which is a public walk almost a mile in length. The river on one hand falls in cascades, and the opposite banks are formed of rich corn-lands; on the other hand, the level meads are bounded by a gentle rising ground covered with wood. One end of this walk is terminated by lofty rocks scattered over with trees; the other by the ruins of the castle impending over the river, by a bridge of two arches, and the town of Derwent hanging on the distant hill. [81]

The appearance of the country is picturesque, and pleasantly diversified with hill and dale, rocks, woodlands and water, enclosures and open grounds. The lands consist of about one half in cultivation, and the other half heath and wastes: near the rivers the soil is fertile, in other parts barren; the chief fuel is coal, sold at about three-pence the

[76] *The Universal British Directory of Trade, Commerce, and Manufacture Vol. 2. 1790-98*

[77] Hutchinson, William. 1794 *The History of the County of Cumberland*

[78] Hutchinson, William. 1794 *The History of the County of Cumberland*

[79] Hutchinson, William. 1794 *The History of the County of Cumberland*

[80] Hutchinson, William. 1794 *The History of the County of Cumberland*

[81] *The Universal British Directory of Trade, Commerce, and Manufacture Vol. 2. 1790-98*

Winchester bushel. The great roads lead to Whitehaven, Workington, Keswick, and Hesket. [82]

The principal inns are the Globe, kept by Mr. Jonathan Word; the Sun, Mr. William Antrobus; and the George and Dragon, Mr. William Scott. There is a coach from London to this place from the Bull and Mouth, near Aldersgate-street, daily, at seven in the morning, and one and seven in the afternoon; also from the Saracen's Head, Snow-hill, daily, at half past seven and eight in the morning. [83]

Carriers are Daniel Barnes from Cockermouth to Workington, 7 miles, Wednesday and Saturday, returns the same days.—Abraham Robinson and Thomas Steel, from Cockermouth to Whitehaven, 13 miles, Tuesday, Thursday, and Saturday, return the same days.—Daniel Barnes, from Cockermouth to Maryport, 7 miles, Tuesday and Friday, returns the same days.—Joseph Blaine, from Cockermouth to Carlisle, 28 miles, to Wigton, 18 miles, from Carlisle to Whitehaven, by way of Wigton, Maryport, Cockermouth, Workington, and to Whitehaven, and returns from Whitehaven on Thursday on his route to Carlisle; sets out from Carlisle on Monday, and arrives at Cockermouth on Tuesday evening, at John Steel's, the Ship, and sets out next morning for Whitehaven, and performs this journey once a week.—Wilfrid Robinson goes the same road as Blaine, except Mary-port to Wigton, from the above places. Inns at Mrs. Robinson's, the Pack-horse, Cockermouth.—Samuel Norman, from Cockermouth to Keswick, 12 miles, Monday, Wednesday, and Friday, and returns the same days, sets off at three o'clock in the morning from his own house, the George and Dragon, and stops at the Globe, Cockermouth.—The London stage wagon, by Mr. John Tanson, of the Royal Oak inn, Keswick, from Kendal, by Low Wood, Keswick, Cockermouth, Workington, and Whitehaven, arrives at the Globe inn, Cockermouth, on Tuesday and Friday mornings, at ten o'clock, and proceeds to Workington and Whitehaven, and returns the next day. [84]

Apart from the bailiff, other town officials ensured the smooth running of Cockermouth. Two constables were chosen annually and as a mark of authority wore distinctive three-cornered hats, long coats, short knee breeches and rough hose. At designated public posts in the town the town crier would ring his bell and cry out messages of importance. Numerous assessors were appointed to various roles. Four men assessed house and land value for dues owed to the lord of the manor. Another pair of assessors held responsibility for ensuring the ale and

---

[82] Hutchinson , William. 1794 *The History of the County of Cumberland*

[83] *The Universal British Directory of Trade, Commerce, and Manufacture Vol. 2. 1790-98*

[84] *The Universal British Directory of Trade, Commerce, and Manufacture Vol. 2. 1790-98*

bread produced in the town was of sufficient quality and pricing kept at a reasonable level.[85] No doubt tasting of the ale and bread formed part of the assessment.

Other officials with the lofty title of "lookers" supervised the running of the lord's mill, where tenants were to take their grain and the miller would take a fair share in payment. They also oversaw the markets, impounded animals, inspected boundary lines, looked into the tanneries and identified pigs turned out to find pannage.[86] Pannage was a right or privilege granted to local people where domestic pigs were released on common land, in order that they may feed on fallen acorns, beechmast, chestnuts or other nuts. These men were appointed annually at a court held in the Moot Hall.

The church Vestry provided another means for the townspeople to be involved with the running of Cockermouth. The church was a significant part of people's lives, in not only religious instruction, but education, festivities and significant town matters. The Vestry meeting, run by elected churchwardens, therefore became concerned with public matters such as the setting rates for poor, police, church, and even appointing a highway surveyor.

The town also hosted a Widows' Hospital, founded by the Rev. T. Leathes, Rector of Plumbland, in 1760. It was located on the left hand corner of Mackreth Row, Kirkgate. The endowment was £100, to which his daughter, Elizabeth Winder, in 1775, added £50 more. These sums were invested in consolidated annuities of three per cent and in turnpike shares, the dividends from which amounted to £40. This money was devoted to the use of six poor widows, or other unmarried poor women above sixty years of age. Due to house being only able to accommodate three of the widows the other three resided elsewhere, each receiving £5 4s. per annum.[87]

---

[85] Bradbury, J.Bernard, 1995 Bradbury's History of Cockermouth, Published by Richard Byers.

[86] Bradbury, J.Bernard, 1995 Bradbury's History of Cockermouth, Published by Richard Byers.

[87] *Askew, John. 1866 A guide to the interesting places in and around Cockermouth*

Chapter Six - Isaac Cragg (1770-1858) and Ruth Osburne (1765-1849)

Isaac and Ruth had settled in Cockermouth by June 1794. That month their first child Mary, named after Ruth's sister, was baptized on the 9 June at All Saints Church. However, the exact date of her birth was not included in the register entry.

It is helpful to note that there was a strong tradition in naming children after their parents or grandparents. Alternatives to this pattern may have been the names of Biblical figures, Royalty or other public notables of the day. If a close relative had recently died then a newborn child may be given their name in memorial. Over the next seventeen years, Isaac and Ruth bore another seven children whose baptisms at All Saints Church were recorded. In order they were John (1795 father's father), Jane (1799 mother's sister), Ruth (1801 mother's mother), Joseph (1803 mother's brother), Isaac (1805 father), Solomon (1809 mother's father) and Elizabeth (1810 father's mother, mother's mother's sister or mother's step-mother).

In 1801, the town of Cockermouth had 417 houses occupied by 690 families. In the town lived 1,255 males and 1,610 females. Of these only 101 people were employed in agriculture, whilst 1,545 were employed in manufacturing, trade or handcraft.[88]

By 1811, twelve of Cumberland's towns had 1,000 or more inhabitants each, who constituted 40 percent of the county's population. Cumberland was in the process of exchanging agriculture for industry and trade as the population grew dramatically somewhere between 34.6 and 50 percent between 1750 and 1801. The 1811 census showed Cockermouth now had 602 houses occupied by 709 families. Of these families, 64 were involved in agriculture and 386 in manufacturing, trade or handcraft. The town now had 1,342 males and 1,622 females.[89] Cockermouth quickly became a regional centre with increased coach and wagon traffic passing through, alongside Kendal, Penrith, Whitehaven, Ulveston and Carlisle. Still, in 1821 35.5% of Cumberland's families remained engaged in agriculture.[90] However, in that year 16.5% of Cockermouth's township was engaged in agriculture, despite being up from 9% in 1811. In 1821, Cockermouth had 721 houses occupied by 776 families. Of these families, 128 were involved in agriculture and 613 in manufacturing, trade or handcraft. The town now had

---

[88] Abstract of Answers and Returns under Act for taking Account of Population of Great Britain (Enumeration Abstract), 1801 HOUSE OF COMMONS PAPERS; ACCOUNTS AND PAPERS, Paper 9, VI.1 Page 48.

[89] Abstract of Answers and Returns under Act for taking Account of Population of Great Britain (Enumeration Abstract), 1811 Session:1812, HOUSE OF COMMONS PAPERS; ACCOUNTS AND PAPERS, Paper Number 316, Volume/page: XI.1

[90] C.M.L Bouch and G.P. Jones, *A Short Economic and Social History of the Lake Counties, 1500-1830*, 1961, Manchester University Press.

1,752 males and 2,038 females.[91] Whilst the town had grown in size the ratio of agricultural workers to those working in manufacturing, trade or handcraft industries had stayed relatively the same.

In 1785, Cockermouth had a population of 2,652, comprising of 663 families. By 1851, the population had doubled to 5,775. Fortunately, Isaac and Ruth had chosen an "exceedingly healthy"[92] town to settle in where the average life expectancy was 83 years in 1842.

Market day for the town at that time was on a Monday:

> The market is abundantly stocked with every description of native produce, and to the stranger or tourist is especially well worth a visit. From about 10 o'clock in the morning to 12 at noon, the spacious Markethouse is filled with a dense crowd of townspeople, butchers, farmers, portly farmers' wives, and blooming dairymaids, all eager to make a profitable exchange of their several commodities. Whilst green-grocers, milliners, dyers, Cheap Johns, and other miscellaneous dealers, put forth to the utmost their keenest trading abilities towards turning an honest penny, during the short busy harvest.[93]

Between 1835 and 1838, a Market Hall was erected by John Dent and John Mackreth at a cost £5,190 and considered "one of the most commodious in Cumberland". A private company in which shares could be purchased controlled it. Of the 124 shares worth £25 each, the Earl of Lonsdale purchased £2,000 worth to aid "tradesmen in the decline of life, residing within the township of Cockermouth" who would receive £1 annually.

---

[91] Abstract of Answers and Returns under Act for taking Account of Population of Great Britain (Enumeration Abstract; Parish Register Abstract), 1821, HOUSE OF COMMONS PAPERS; ACCOUNTS AND PAPERS, Paper Number 502, Volume/page XV.1

[92] Directory of Cumberland, 1847

[93] *Askew, John. 1866 A guide to the interesting places in and around Cockermouth*

Figure 23 All Saints Church (David Cragg)

All Saints Church figured prominently in the life of Isaac's family, as it was the most central church in the town, both socially and administratively. A church had been sitting on the hill overlooking the town since the reign of Edward III (1327-77). Rebuilt in 1711, it had been later enlarged and improved in 1825.

> It is now a commodious edifice, surmounted by a steeple, containing a peel of six bells, with a clock and chimes; the curacy is perpetual, in the gift of the Earl of Lonsdale, and the Rev. Edward Fawcett is the present curate. [94]

Edward Fawcett was the perpetual curate of All Saints from 1809 until 1864, when he died on 24 February that year at 86 years of age.[95] The most dramatic reconstruction of All Saints was completed between February 1852 and June 1854 after the church burnt down when a stove overheated on Friday 15 November 1850. However, the endeavour was not without controversy over the choice of design, and the removal of 100 graves caused an uproar.

---

[94] Pigots 1830 Directory.

[95] *Clergy of The Church of England Database,*
http://www.theclergydatabase.org.uk/jsp/persons/DisplayPerson.jsp?PersonID=5848, last accessed 16/09/2013

REMAINS OF COCKERMOUTH CHURCH.

Figure 24 All Saints Church after the 1850 fire (London Illustrated News)[96]

When finally reopened on 15 June 1854, Dr Graham, Bishop of Chester consecrated All Saints. The new building was:

> ...cruciform in shape, having a nave, aisles, transepts, chancel, and tower, which, with the spire, has an elevation of 180 feet. The style is early English, or as it is sometimes termed modern Gothic, from a design by Joseph Clark, Esq., Architect, of London. The east window, which is of stained glass, emblazoned with scripture worthies, is a subscription memorial to the Poet "Wordsworth. A brass tablet on the north-east pier of the tower, within the chancel, has this fact engraven upon it as follows :

> "To the Glory of God and the honoured memory of "William Wordsworth, Poet Laureate, the east window of this Church is raised in this his native place, by public subscription, A.D., 1853." [97]

Within the church, numbered church pews, decorated with personal cushions and carpet, were bought and sold, sometimes at a profit. A midwife was licensed to All Saints, whose role included the supervision of baptisms.

---

[96] "Remains of Cockermouth Church." Illustrated London News [London, England] 30 Nov. 1850: 416. Illustrated London News. Web. 13 Oct. 2013

[97] Askew, John. 1866 *A guide to the interesting places in and around Cockermouth*

The graveyard adjacent to the church includes the bodies of plague victims from 1647, however it has also been said that the victims are buried at Hundith Hill crossroads.[98] Next to the graveyard are the Church Rooms. In Isaac's day the Free Grammar School, founded in 1676 stood there instead. Both Wordsworth and Fletcher Christian were students at this school. In the upper room, a Sunday School was held for poor employed children who were taught reading and writing, by a paid teacher.[99] By 1829, there were three Sunday schools with 600 pupils, attached to All Saints, Methodist and Independent Chapels.[100] In 1806 a School of Industry was established in the town for 30 poor girls where knitting and sewing were taught alongside the traditional reading, writing and arithmetic. By 1847, there were numerous schools in Cockermouth, including the Grammar School, National School and the British School.

The Grammar School (serving both Cockermouth and Embleton), located in All Saints' Churchyard, was founded by Philip Lord Wharton, Sir George Fletcher, Sir Richard Graham, and Doctor Smith the Bishop of Carlisle, in 1679. The endowment in 1866 was about £25 per annum, derived from tithes, house rents, dividends on stock, and an annual payment of 6s. 8d. from Embleton.[101]

The National School, erected in 1845 was situated in New Street, and established through the exertions of the Rev. Charles Southey, son of the poet Robert Southey. In 1866, it was considered "a good substantial building, capable of accommodating about 220 children".[102]

In South Street, a General Sunday School was established in 1832. It was observed to be "a commodious" two storey building capable of accommodating 400 children. Established chiefly through the exertions of the John Richardson, brewer, who was superintendent of the institution for 26 years. On the afternoon of the Sunday it was first used, the upper storey was bursting at the seams with scholars. Unfortunately, the floor supports were unable to hold the weight and gave way, "dragging down with it a partition staircase-wall, which fell inwards upon the children below, crushing two of them to death".[103]

---

[98] Bradbury, J.Bernard, 1995 Bradbury's History of Cockermouth, Published by Richard Byers.

[99] H. E. Winter, Cockermouth (A History and Guide), 1992

[100] W. Parson and W. White, History, Directory and Gazetteer of the Counties of Cumberland and Westmorland. (Leeds 1829).

[101] *Askew, John. 1866 A guide to the interesting places in and around Cockermouth*

[102] *Askew, John. 1866 A guide to the interesting places in and around Cockermouth*

[103] *Askew, John. 1866 A guide to the interesting places in and around Cockermouth*

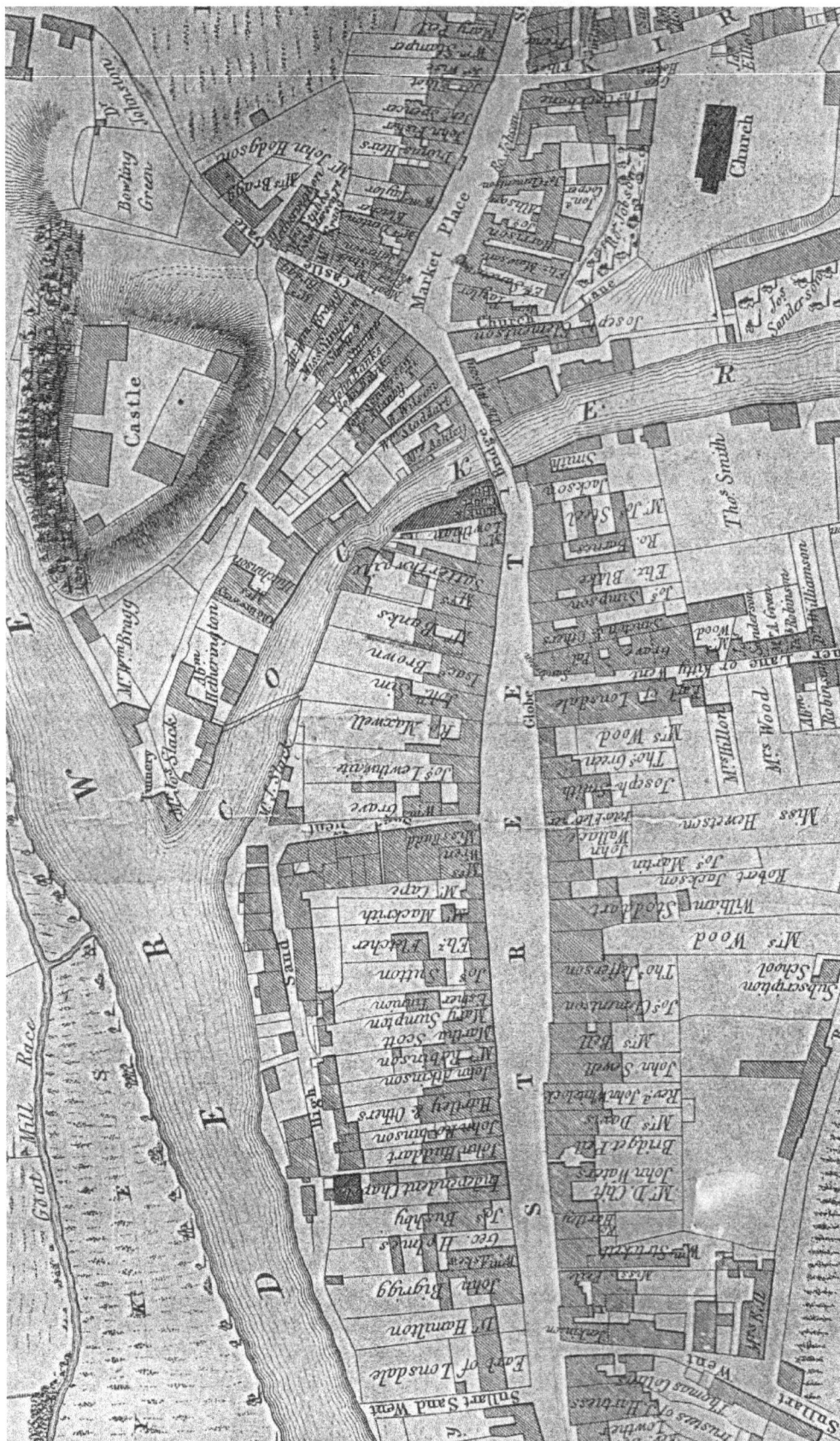

Figure 25 Extract from John Wood's 1832 map of Cockermouth (Cumbria Record Office ref. D/Lec. Plans)

Isaac was a serving man in Workington, but in Cockermouth, he declared himself to be a husbandman (tenant farmer) for the baptism of his daughter Ruth in 1801. As a tenant farmer, Isaac may have leased and worked on land owned by the Earl of Egremont who was lord of the manor. The map of Cockermouth 1775 by Hodkinson and Donald (see Figure 21) shows the extent of common land 25 years prior. Between 1793 and 1816, 200,000 acres of commons were enclosed in Cumberland.[104] As a result, by 1829, 7,222 farms existed in Cumberland and about 4,559 of these were leased by tenants such as Isaac.[105] A Board of Agriculture Report written in 1794 gives some insights into the nature of farming in Cumberland around the time Isaac would have taken up his tenement in Cockermouth:

> 'There are probably few counties where property in land is divided into such small parcels as in Cumberland and those small properties so universally occupied by the owners, by far the greatest part of which are held under the lords of the manors, by that species of vassalage, called customary tenure, subject to the payment of fines and heriots on alienation, the death of the lord...or the tenant, and the payment of certain annual rents, and the performance of various services called Boondays, such as getting and leading the lord's peats, plowing and harrowing his land, reaping his corn, haymaking, carrying letters etc., whenever summoned by the lord. We cannot pretend to be accurate, but believe that two thirds of the county are held by this kind of tenure in tenements from £5 to £50 a year, but the generality are from £15 to £30.'[106]

Cultivation of the land by Cumberland's inhabitants came under the critical eye of numerous expert commentators who tended to agree that backwardness and poor land management contributed to poor crops yields. However, the weather was less kind to farmers in the north of England than in the south. One such reminiscent commentator, William Dickinson remarked in 1876 that:

> Their crops consisted chiefly then in barley, oats and hay; Some rye was sown, some beans and peas, But these in a small degree; And both on small and middling farms there was no wheat to see.[107]

Men's wages on average in 1795 were £10 a year, and women's £4.[108] Later on Isaac must have given away farming, and found the wage of a tanner more attractive. The agricultural depression following Waterloo and marked fall in prices after 1820 most likely encouraged

---

[104] Second Report, Commission on the Employment of Children, Young Persons and Women in Agricultural (1867).

[105] C.M.L Bouch and G.P. Jones, The Lake Counties, 1500-1800 by, 1961, Manchester University Press.

[106] E. Hughes, North County Life in the Eighteenth Century, Vol II. 1965, University of Durham, Great Britian

[107] William Dickinson, Cumbriana, 2nd Edition, 1876

[108] Hutchinson, History of Cumberland, 1795

this transition as well of the development of housing and industry on enclosed town land. Tanning was first listed as Isaac's trade in the 1841 census, and again in his death certificate in 1858. In choosing tanning as a trade, Isaac unknowingly initiated an employment trend within the family that would exist for the next century and a half. A tanner would treat animal skins making them into leather. An extract of the bark from oak trees, called 'tannins' would help preserve the skin keeping it pliable and strong. A local windmill in Cockermouth would crush the bark to extract the tannin. Once the tannin was mixed with water, the skin was soaked in this mixture in a pit for a considerable length of time, sometimes months.[109] Cockermouth was second only to Kendal in the tanning trade in Cumberland.[110]

By 1820, the signs of modernisation and prosperity began to show markedly in Cockermouth:

> ...a row of low thatched houses occupied part of Main Street, but were replaced by 1866 by the Railway Hotel, King's Arms Inn, and the modernized shops of Ingham, Youdale, and Graham. The Appletree Inn was then a thatched tavern. The old unsightly Moot Hall continued to stand on the open space at the foot of Castle Street. The Savings Bank of Cockermouth was established in 1818. A high and dangerous old bridge of 15 feet road-way, spanned the Cocker at mid-town, and one equally dangerous, of 12 feet, road-way, crossed the Derwent at the Goat suburb.

Figure 26 Cockermouth Bridge at Goat Suburb and Castle 1822 - T Fielding/Thomas Maclean (Cumbria Images)

---

[109] Museum of Lakeland Life and Industry, Kendal, Cumbria, England.
[110] H. E. Winter, Cockermouth (A History and Guide), 1992.

Figure 27 Old Moot Hall (Cumbria Images)

The handsome bridge, which now spans the Derwent, was erected in 1820, at a cost of £3,000. The old Moot Hall and Butchers' Shambles, thereto attached, were pulled down in 1827. Cocker Bridge, the Court House, Messrs. Irwin & Fawcett's shop, &c, were erected in 1828-1829. The stones from the Moot Hall were used for the Court House. This bridge cost £2,500.[111]

On 3 December 1820, Isaac Cragg was amongst a party of men indulging in an illegal activity on the banks of the Derwent River at Isel about 10km north-east of Cockermouth.

**Figure 28 St Michael and All Angels' Church, Isel and the Derwent River.
Aerial photo by Simon Ledingham.**

---

[111] *Askew, John. 1866 A guide to the interesting places in and around Cockermouth*

A Caution.-—On Sunday, the 3rd inst., a set of daring and profligate poachers, calling themselves fishermen, had the audacity, during the performance of Divine Service, and within a hundred yards the church at Isell, to commence drawing for salmon in the river. As soon as the congregation were dismissed, Thomas Wybergh, Esq magistrate [of] this county, with some assistance, attempted [to] surround the party, many of whom fled at his approach; but one Isaac Cragg, of Cockermouth, tanner, and John Garley, the same place, mason, were secured. They had taken four large salmon, and had two nets which were immediately cut to pieces by order of the magistrate, and the salmon were divided and distributed as directed by Act of Parliament; the two offenders were permitted to depart, upon their undertaking to appear on Tuesday, the inst., before Mr. Wybergh, at Isell Hall, which day they were severally convicted in the penalty of five pounds - Whitehaven Gazette.[112]

Poaching to a certain extent was brought on by the land enclosures, which was the taking of common land and converting to various other uses by the gentry. One such "Inclosure Bill" had been passed by Parliament on 10 May 1813 for "inclosing lands in the Borough and Township of Cockermouth".[113] It had first been introduced to Parliament on 8 March 1813 by Sir Charles Merrik Burrell. Poaching had been going on since the 14th century in many forms, but reached a peak between about 1750 and 1850, with various parliamentary acts making it increasingly difficult to undertake legally. As a result, areas where people in the past had been free to farm and hunt game were now off limits, they had lost much of the land they used and had become tenants rather than using common land so food was scarcer. This generally drove

Figure 29 Isel Hall on the Derwent River.
Aerial photo by Simon Ledingham

---

[112] *Westmorland Gazette* - Saturday 16 December 1820

[113] Journals of the House of Commons 1688-1834, 24 November 1812 - 1 November 1813

tenants to poaching in order to survive. There were of course professional gangs of poachers as well supplying the towns.

Between 1750 and about 1820, a poacher could expect to be hanged (if they used a firearm) or transported to Australia for 14 years if convicted, so Isaac got off lightly for his transgressions. The Poaching Prevention Act 1862 allowed police to stop and search anyone suspected of carrying poaching implements.

It was not until 1883 when an act of Parliament allowed tenant farmers to kill rabbits and hares on their rented land were the levels of illegal poaching significantly reduced. However, the penalties for poaching still remained at up to 7 years hard labour or transportation to a penal colony. Therefore, the six salmon that Isaac had in his possession could hardly have been for his own use. To receive only two months for the offense suggests a very lenient magistrate, or the owner of the property he poached from did not press for a hard sentence. Perhaps Isaac actually worked for the landowner and his services were too valuable to lose.

December was an extremely popular time of the year for desperate and opportunistic poachers in Cumberland in the 1800s, as most outdoor agricultural work was disrupted during winter. This peak poaching time was also influenced by the winter breeding patterns of salmon, when adult salmon could be easily obtained. A study of salmon poaching prosecutions on the Derwent between 1880 and 1882 showed that 45% to 50% of them occurred during December.[114] During reproduction, typically occurring in December, salmon assemble on their spawning beds in the shallow and narrow streams of the upper Derwent River. At this stage, the fish are often gathered in large numbers and usually become much more visible, than in months prior.[115] Contemporary accounts claimed, for example, that such was the density of salmon on the spawning redds of the Cumberland Derwent at times that it was often possible to 'see literally dozens of salmon fins out of the water'.[116]

Some poachers, together with their family, consumed the salmon they caught, but others poached for profit, hawking the fish directly within their own neighbourhood.[117] One poacher's claim 'that when work is not always to be had for the asking, the fish are then the

---

[114] Osborne, Harvey. 2000 *"The seasonality of nineteenth-century poaching"* British Agricultural History Review Volume 48, Part 1, pp27-41 http://www.bahs.org.uk/AGHR/ARTICLES/48n1a2.pdf

[115] Osborne, Harvey. 2000 *"The seasonality of nineteenth-century poaching"* British Agricultural History Review Volume 48, Part 1, pp27-41 http://www.bahs.org.uk/AGHR/ARTICLES/48n1a2.pdf

[116] Thistlethwaite, June. 1997 *Cumbrian Women Remember*, p. 180

[117] Osborne, Harvey. 2000 *"The seasonality of nineteenth-century poaching"* British Agricultural History Review Volume 48, Part 1, pp27-41 http://www.bahs.org.uk/AGHR/ARTICLES/48n1a2.pdf

most plentiful', helps demonstrate how important the arrival of the adult salmon to spawn was to making poaching a viable response to winter poverty.[118]

In the town, a Gas Works was established in 1834, at a cost of £3,000 in £5 shares. By 1836, the Vestry had reached contractual terms with the gas company and the streets of Cockermouth were lit. In 1856, the works were enlarged at a further cost of £3,000 subscribed by the shareholders.[119] Electricity was eventually introduced to the town in 1881.

The 1841 census was the first detailed census to be taken in England and Wales. Fortunately, the Cragg family are not difficult to locate as Isaac and his family were still residing in Cockermouth on 6 June 1841. Isaac and Ruth lived in the last house on Sand Went (now called High Sand Lane), just before High Sand (now known as Waterloo Street). At the back of the house, just beyond the yard, the Cocker River flowed into the Derwent River. The Castle Tannery operated across the river, as well as the Richardson tannery where Isaac was working. Unfortunately, many of the original houses do not still stand in this street, as they have either been refurbished or replaced.

The land close to where they lived on was enclosed in 1818.[120]

Cockermouth Inclosure.

TO be SOLD in Public Sale, on THURS-DAY the 27th Day of August, 1818, at the *Globe Inn*, in Cockermouth, by Order of the COMMISSIONERS appointed by an Act of Parliament lately passed, intituled "An Act for inclosing Lands in the Borough and Township of *COCKERMOUTH*, in the County of Cumberland," either Together, or in the following or other Lots, as may be fixed at the Time of Sale,— The following Parcels of Freehold Land, Parts of the Common directed to be inclosed by the said Act, as the same are now set out, *namely*,

---

[118] Denwood, Cumbrian nights, p. 60

[119] *Askew, John. 1866 A guide to the interesting places in and around Cockermouth*

[120] Cumberland Pacquet, and Ware's Whitehaven Advertiser - Tuesday 04 August 1818

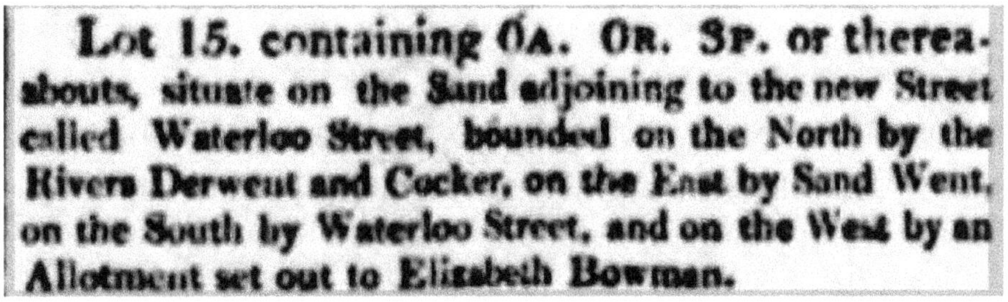

> Lot 15. containing 0A. 0R. 3P. or thereabouts, situate on the Sand adjoining to the new Street called Waterloo Street, bounded on the North by the Rivers Derwent and Cocker, on the East by Sand Went, on the South by Waterloo Street, and on the West by an Allotment set out to Elizabeth Bowman.

Waterloo Street, which runs parallel to banks of the Derwent, was formerly known as simply as "The Sands", as it was once open land, which extended 'above Cocker foot' along the bank of the Cocker. Twenty years before Isaac and Ruth arrived in Cockermouth development along Sand Went had begun to spread around the corner to the "The Sands". Hodkinson and Donald's 1775 Map of Cockermouth (Figure 20) shows this progress. By 1832, development on both sides of High Sand had resulted in a built up area. Buildings on the southern side of the street were often at the foot of Main Street gardens, suggesting the same owner had buildings facing Main Street and High Sand.

This census also tells us that both Isaac and Ruth were born in the county of Cumberland, and had their forty year old daughter Sarah living with them, as well as two visitors.

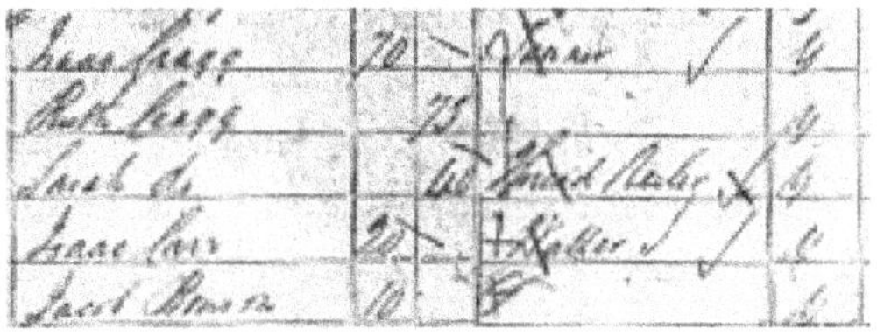

Figure 30 1841 Census entry for Isaac Cragg's household in Sand Went, Cockermouth

The census had an unusual way of recording ages, as the census collectors were instructed to:

> 'write down the age of every person under 15 years of age as it was stated to you. For persons aged 15 years and upwards, write the lowest of the term of 5 years within the age is reached.'

Thus, a person 34 years of age was recorded as 30. This makes it difficult to ascertain a person's correct age. The census states that Isaac was between 70 and 74 years of age, which fits with him being born in 1770 and being 4 months away from his 71st birthday. Ruth however, was recorded as between 75 and 79 years of age. This agrees with her death certificate that states she was 84 in 1849, which means she was born in 1765. Ruth states in the census that she was born in the county of Cumberland, and the only known christening of a Ruth Osborn around that time was in 1771. This can be explained though, as her parents were married in 1763, and she may have been christened as a child rather than as an infant.

By 1841, as a tanner Isaac's strength had become legendary and even made page two of the *Cumberland Pacquet, and Ware's Whitehaven Advertiser* on Tuesday 13 July 1841. The reported and slightly exaggerated age of 84 however suggests that he was born in 1757!

> On Thursday last a man of the olden time named Isaac Cragg, in the employ of Mr. Richardson, tanner, Cockermouth, who has attained the goodly age of 84 years, carried a bark-sack containing 29 stone of oats, upon his back across the tan-yard, and afterwards ascended a flight of 28 steps into the granary with his ponderous load, which he emptied into the corn-chest. This extraordinary feat was performed the Herculean octogenarian without his ever once resting, and even after its accomplishment he appeared to very little fatigued.[121]

There were a few Richardson's living in Cockermouth in 1841. Isaac's employer was John Richardson junior, a tanner of 20 to 24 years of age, who lived in Brewery Yard, on Brewery Lane with his young family. Off Brewery Lane where the Derwent and Cocker Rivers converged, there were a number of tanneries operating. Bark sacks typically held bark to be used in the tanning process, after a local mill, such as Little Mill, had ground the bark. However, in this case the bark sacks contained oats. A windmill did also exist on Brewery Lane amongst the tanneries. John Richardson junior was fortunate that his father, John Richardson, was the local brewer who occupied the Old Brewery and house next door. By virtue of their annual rents exceeding £50, both Richardson men were two of the 217 Cockermouth men entitled to vote in the 1841 general election.[122]

During the period of industrialisation, Cockermouth had developed many narrow courtyards and alleys inhabited by small workshops, mills, tanneries, foundries and dye-works in which the workers and artisans lived cheek-by-jowl with their work place, in quite appalling squalor.[123] In 1847, discussion at a Vestry meeting in the town centred on the need for a Local Act to improve paving, lighting, watching, cleansing and general improvement of the township. However, it stopped short of the need to agitate for a more adequate drainage and sewer system for the town. This meeting ultimately resulted in the proposal of the Cockermouth Improvement Bill. An enquiry was held at the Globe Inn headed by two commissioners from London, John Job Rawlinson and William Hosking. The Reverend Edward Fawcett was in support of the Bill whilst Lieutenant-General Wyndham was against,

---

[121]Cumberland Pacquet, and Ware's Whitehaven Advertiser - Tuesday 13 July 1841

[122] Cockermouth Elector's Lists 1 December 1840

[123] http://www.derwentfells.com/pdfs/journal/Newsletter24.pdf, last accessed Oct 2 2013

primarily due to cost considerations. In the resulting eight-page report, the Commissioners found: [124]

> There is at present nothing which can rightly be denominated as a sewer in the town, and consequently there are no drains to carry off the refuse and ordure from the houses into common sewers.

> The town is wholly unsewered except by the rivers, and by becks and mountain torrents, which latter are greatly diminished, and sometimes wholly fail in the Summer season.

> Wherever houses are upon one of the rivers or upon one of the becks, the margins of the stream are covered with human excrement, which falls from the privates jutting out from the houses and overhanging the beds of the water courses. In the summer when the streams are low, the accumulations must be great, inasmuch as on a wet winter day the margins of all the streams in and through the town were much befouled.

> The narrow and winding alleys north-west of the Market-Place and immediately under the walls of the Castle …were brimming with their filthy contents and a cluster of privies for the common service of some houses at a place called Camperdown were found to be as revoltingly offensive in their exposure as in their foulness".

> The footways of the town of Cockermouth are roughly paved and ill kept – that the streets are often in a dirty state from the duties of the scavenger being ill performed.

Their conclusion however was that:

> We are of opinion, that the Promoters of the Bill have shown no special reasons why such a Bill as they were soliciting should be passed into law.

The Commissioners confirmed that the Bill as it stood was insufficient to address the more pressing drainage and sewage issues the town had. The Bill was consequently dropped. Hope was then placed in a latter more general bill such as the Health of Towns Act, 1848 and Local Government Act, 1858.

It was no surprise then, that two years later, at the height of summer in July 1849 Cockermouth was hit heavily by the cholera pandemic that was sweeping across Europe. In the township, at least 20 deaths from cholera and 6 from diarrhoea had been recorded by 30 September.[125] That year in England and Wales 53,293 cholera deaths were recorded. Of the 419 cholera related deaths, which occurred in Cumberland, the Cockermouth Registration District (including the towns of Maryport, Keswick and Workington) accounted for 282 deaths whilst

[124] J B Bradbury "A History of Cockermouth", Phillimore, 1995 p77.
[125] *Justice of the Peace*, Volume 13, 1849. London, Published by Henry Shaw.

Carlisle and Whitehaven only had 51 and 79 respectively.[126] By 1855, the number of deaths from this disease fell below "average" in Cockermouth and Workington to 25 deaths per quarter.[127] Cholera had previously visited Cockermouth in 1832. The victims at that time had been buried in a mass grave near the Kirkgate entrance to All Saints Church yard.

A report prepared by the Registrar General, George Graham for the Home Secretary, Sir George Grey titled *Report on the mortality of cholera in England, 1848-49* was issued in 1852.[128] It contained a breakdown by Town of the deaths caused by the epidemic in the Cockermouth Registration District (See Table 1). Cockermouth was considered at that time one of the most fatal registration districts in England.

Table 1 Cholera Related Deaths in Cockermouth Registration District 1848-49

Town	Population	Cholera	Diarrhoea	Comments
Keswick	6001	5	0	First, death from cholera took place on June 25th; last death on September 11th, a weaver's wife, aged 30.
Cockermouth	9491	60	11	After a prevalence of diarrhoea, the first death from cholera happened to a sempstress, aged 60, at St. Helens-street, where several other deaths took place: in Main-street, Waterloo-street, Skinner-street, and Papcastle, many fatal cases occurred. The last, death was that of a draper's son, aged 3 years, at Crown-street, November 4th.
Workington	9424	167	14	Cholera was first fatal to a blacksmith at the Quay, on 9th August. The epidemic prevailed severely at Priest-gate, in Powstreet, Church street and lane, Griffin-street, and Brow Top. The families of mariners and coalminers suffered greatly. The last death was that of a labourer's wife, aged 51, on November 8th, at Camerton.
Maryport	10774	50	2	The first death registered from cholera was that of a sailor, who died at sea, in the passage between Dublin and Maryport: this was followed by the death of a blacksmith, aged 47, at Furnace-road, August 9th. More than one-fourth of the deaths took place in Kirby-street; several also occurred in Furnace-lane, Crosby-street, and Queenstreet; the last on November

[126] A History of Epidemics in Britain, Volume 1, Charles Creighton, 1965.

[127] *Justice of the Peace*, Volume 19, 1855. London, Published by Henry Shaw

[128] Great Britain. Report on the mortality of cholera in England, 1848-49. London : Printed by W. Clowes, for H.M.S.O., 1852. http://pds.lib.harvard.edu/pds/view/8278007?n=429

Town	Population	Cholera	Diarrhoea	Comments
				12th, when a ship-Wright's son, aged 9 years, died at Senhouse-street.

Ruth Cragg passed away on 15 December 1849. Just one month after the last cholera related death was officially recorded. The *Cumberland Pacquet* published the following obituary on Tuesday 18 December 1849.

> Ruth, the wife of Mr. Isaac Cragg, tanner, aged 84 years. The deceased has left a husband, who is in his 83d year, and likewise children, grand-children, and great grand-children, amounting in the whole to no less than sixty.[129]

Sixty descendants in her lifetime was a significant achievement for Ruth and Isaac. She died at their residence (shared with John Cragg's family) at the end of Sand Lane (renaming of Sand Went), in Cockermouth, at the age of 84. Their street joined onto Waterloo Street and Main Street where the majority of recent deaths had occurred. The cause of death was listed as '12 hours of diarrhea[sic]', but no doctor was present at the time of her passing. Joseph, their son, however was present at Ruth's death, though he lived in Brewery Lane near the castle. The eldest son John Cragg had already passed away in January that year. Her death was highly likely the result of the cholera outbreak as chronic diarrhoea was a major symptom. That same year Solomon Cragg's daughter Elizabeth Cragg also passed away in the June quarter at age 17. Once again, the likely cause was the cholera.

[129] Cumberland Pacquet, and Ware's Whitehaven Advertiser - Tuesday 18 December 1849

Figure 31 Part of Survey Map of Cockermouth 1832 by John Wood for the Earl of Egremont. Includes Sand Went and Brewery Lane

Figure 32 Cockermouth Town Centre Today (Google Maps)

After Ruth's death, Isaac may have left Cockermouth to live with one of his children in Bridekirk parish or nearby Brigham. As his son John and wife Ruth had both passed away during 1849 at the Sand Lane address he probably decided it was time to move on. We know he was not in Cockermouth in 1851, as the census does not record him residing there, on the night it was taken. In this census Isaac's son Solomon Craigg[sic] (Railway Labourer) and his wife Elizabeth (an Inn Keeper), were living in the village of Dearham with no children. The 1847 Directory of Cumberland lists Solomon Craigg[sic] as the Victualler of Queen's Head (Inn) in Dearham. The Directory also remarks that the Parish of Dearham is known for its "excellent crops of wheat and corn, &c. Coal is raised here in abundance and shipped to Maryport for the Irish market." The township of Dearham "has a village situated 2 ½ miles E. of Maryport, and in 1841 contained 1037 inhabitants."

In a letter written in 1927, John Cragg (born 1855 to Joseph and Sarah) described his Great-Grandfather Isaac.

> *"he used to wear knee breeches, yellow stockings and buckles on his shoes; he was a quaint old man, very interesting. His mind was clear up to when he passed away'.*

It is in Dearham that Isaac is found in 1858, though he was not listed as living there in 1851. Both Solomon and Elizabeth were present at Isaac's death in Dearham on 28 November 1858. Isaac was 92 years of age at time. The cause was judged as simply 'old age'. The age of 92 presents another problem regarding when he was born, similar to his wife's situation. If he were really 92 then he would have been born in 1766, and would have been 4 years old when he was christened in the Poor House. Unfortunately, this still places him in the correct age bracket for the 1841 census (70-74 years old) if he had not yet had his birthday that year. So the 1841 census cannot be used for the verification of Isaac's birthdate. The 1851 census would give the final answer, if only his whereabouts in 1851 could be established. According to the 1928 letter by John, Isaac was buried in the Churchyard in Cockermouth.

Cockermouth was renowned at that time for the longevity of its inhabitants:

> A few days ago, four venerable inhabitants of Cockermouth accidentally met upon the new road leading from that town to Keswick, whose united ages amounted to 335 years! The following are the names and respective ages of the venerable patriarch's alluded to :--Joseph Steel, Esq., aged .96 years ; Mr. Jos. Tiffin, aged 84 years; Mr. John Tyson, aged 83 years; and Mr. Henry Moncrief, aged 82 years. These worthy old gentlemen were all in the act of taking a walk for the benefit of their respective healths (which, it seems, they have attended to with some effect) at the time when they met with each other on the road we have mentioned. There are at this time great number of individuals resident the borough of Cockermouth, whose ages very from 80 to 96 years. Only last week, Mr. Joseph Clemestson, of that borough, who is now in the 94th

year of age purchased new suit clothes, and also provided himself with new stock of linen. Such remarkable instances of longevity as these, we apprehend, are rarely to be met with in any other part of the kingdom, and they certainly speak strongly in favour of the salubrity of Cockermouth.[130]

Only two years before his death a new cemetery was opened in June 1856, and consecrated by the Bishop of Carlisle on September 12. It contained over five acres, and housed two neat Chapels in the early English style of architecture. The total cost, including the keeper's residence, was about £2,800. [131]

---

[130] Cumberland Pacquet, and Ware's Whitehaven Advertiser - Tuesday 30 January 1844

[131] *Askew, John. 1866 A guide to the interesting places in and around Cockermouth*

Chapter Seven - John Cragg (1795-1849) and Jane Oswald (1796-1872)

Of Isaac and Ruth's sons, only John and Joseph chose to stay in Cockermouth. Joseph's line is more relevant to the Cragg family in Australia, as eventually his son Henry brought his family to the antipodes. However, John's own family in Cockermouth is worth looking into, as both families would have lived side by side in the town.

John, born 17 July 1795, in Cockermouth, was Isaac's first son and second child. He was christened on 28 February 1796 in All Saints Church. On 12 November 1815, John married by banns, Jane Oswald in Brigham Parish (which included the town of Cockermouth). Jane was also from the town of Cockermouth. In the marriage register entry John signed his name, which indicated he was able to write and most likely read as well. The benefits of a local education.

The marriage register entry states that John was a 'waller' by trade. This was consistently reported as his trade for his children's baptisms and their marriage register entries up to 1845. As mentioned previously, there are miles and miles of dry-stone walls winding their way across the hills and vales of the Lake District. John Cragg would have had a hand in building these for well over 30 years.

> '...these stone fences were constructed by bands of itinerant wallers who camped out on the fellsides for weeks on end, working from sunrise to sunset and coming down to the valley only on Saturdays. Conditions were harsh and wages pitifully low. ...Although the wallers were skilled craftsmen, most of them were illiterate and unable to write their names.'[132]

The drystone walls were a direct result of the land enclosures. Between 1760 and the start of the French Wars, and then from the early 1800s until 1816 the dry stonewalls increasing divided the land and required bands of wallers to feverishly construct them. The peak period for Cumberland was between 1793 and 1816. By the early 1820s, the Cumberland countryside was a mixture of arable land well ploughed and land left untilled and rough.[133]

---

[132] William Rollinson, A History of Cumberland and Westmorland, 1978, Phillimore & Co. Ltd., Chichester, Sussex, England.

[133] Marshall, J. D. (John Duncan) & Walton, John K 1981, *The Lake Counties from 1830 to the mid-twentieth century : a study in regional change,* Manchester University Press, Manchester [Great Manchester]

Figure 33 Stonewalls in the Lake District (David Cragg)

Jane gave birth to seven children between 1817 and 1839. In order, they were Ruth, Elizabeth, Isaac, John, Jane, Sarah, Solomon and Thomas. Once again, the tradition of naming children after relatives is evident. Their son Solomon later appears in the 1881 census.

Like his father Isaac, John turned to poaching to provide an income and simply put food on the table during times where little or no work was available. Also like Isaac, detection and arrest was only a matter of time. However, the price John paid was much higher in February 1834, some 24 years after his Isaac was fined £5.

> LOCAL INTELLIGENCE. Poaching.—Thomas Gibson and Isaac Barnes, weavers, of Cockermouth. Have been convicted before R. Watts, Esq., Clifton, in the penalty of 50s. each, for having fish in their possession. Jonathan Wilkinson, shoemaker, who was proved to have taken trout from the river with an illegal net, has been committed Carlisle gaol for three months. The following convictions have also taken place before the Rev. E Fawcett: Stephen Coats, labourer, and H. Thompson, mariner, charged with killing fish the river Derwent were fined 50s. each, and in default of payment, the latter has been committed the house correction for two months; John Bigrigg, John Copeland, and Daniel Briscoe, weavers, for similar offences, have been committed to Carlisle gaol for three months. Jacob Carruthers and Wm. Bowes, weavers, and John Cragg, waller, were also convicted before the Petty Sessions in Cockermouth, of killing

fish. The two former have been committed for one month, and the latter for six weeks imprisonment, in the house of correction.[134]

Eight years later on Monday December 12th 1842 John's 21 year-old son Isaac was sentenced after his conviction for a similar offence. Three generations caught poaching!

> At Cockermouth Petty Sessions, ...held on Monday last, Isaac Cragg, a waller, was committed to hard labour in Carlisle gaol for two months, for having six salmon and two nets in his possession, in a field near the Fitz Mill, adjoining the river Derwent.[135]

The demand for wallers had diminished after the 1830s, since the rush to enclose land had effectively ended. Fitz Mill on the River Derwent, where the offence occurred was located on the west bank of the River Derwent where the river takes a sharp bend to the north of the Goat. The Goat (or Gote) was an isolated community separated from the town by fields in which flax retting took place. There had been a mill on this site since at least the late 18th century, and the mill that was standing until around 1980 is believed to have been erected in 1794 as a flax mill. A section of wall and some foundations are all that remain.[136]

Figure 34 Fitz Mill (http://www.cockermouth.org.uk/watermills2012.pdf)

The Petty Sessions at Cockermouth were held from 1833 onwards, following the formation of the Derwent Petty Sessional Division from an amalgamation of parishes in the wards of Allerdale above and below Derwent at the Easter Quarter Sessions of that year.[137]

---

[134] Carlisle Journal - Saturday 15 February 1834

[135] Carlisle Journal - Saturday 17 December 1842

[136] 2012 *The WaterMills of Cockermouth* http://www.cockermouth.org.uk/watermills2012.pdf, last accessed 11 Aug 2013

[137] Records of Cumberland Quarter Sessions [QAA/1 - QPWC/288]
http://www.nationalarchives.gov.uk/a2a/records.aspx?cat=023-cumqs_2&cid=-1#-1, last accessed August 11 2013.

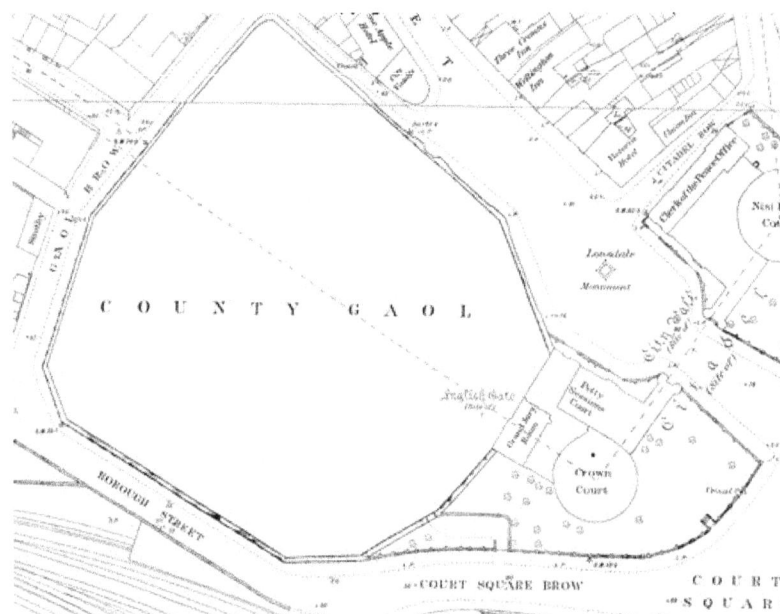

Figure 35 County Gaol 1866 Carlisle Town Plan

Both John and Isaac had been confined to the County Goal in Carlisle. The Cumberland County Goal in Carlisle was also known as the citadel and included two imposing red sandstone towers built by Henry VIII in 1541 to strengthen the defences. Rebuilt in 1810, the west tower (left most tower in the figure below), closest to the railway station, held criminal trials and the goal, the east tower held civil trials.

Figure 36 "Entrance to Carlisle from the South" engraved by E.Finden after a picture by W.Westall, published in Great Britain Illustrated, 1830

The land to the north of the west tower was probably all part of the gaol, the gaol yard and prison hospital, but has more recently been redeveloped into offices and shops.

Just three months prior to his imprisonment, young Isaac had taken part in an annual two day wrestling and sports event in Cockermouth. Held in a field near the Castle, the event spanned across both Friday and Saturday. Apart from wrestling, there was a dog race, which ran over a number of miles and a foot race. In the all-weight wrestling contest Isaac was knocked out in the second round by a Joseph Pearson of Lorton. However, the next day he entered the light-weight wrestling - for men not exceeding eleven stone (i.e. 68kg). He managed to defeat both George Bell from Allerby and William Coulthard, but fell to George Donaldson who eventually won the competition and the £5 prize after "grassing" his own brother Thomas.[138]

The tradition of wrestling was, and still is, popular in Cumberland. It is thought to have evolved from Norse wrestling brought over by Viking invaders or developed from an older Celtic tradition. The starting *backhold* position involved the wrestlers standing chest to chest, grasping each other around the body with their chins on their opponent's right shoulder. The right arm of each contestant was positioned under his opponent's left arm. Once the grip was taken the umpire would give the signal to start the contest by calling "en guard", then "wrestle". The wrestlers would then attempt to unbalance their opponent, or make them lose their hold, using methods such as lifting throws known as "hipes", twisting throws such as "buttocks" and trips like the inside click, cross click, back heel or outside stroke. This is known as a "fall". If any part of a wrestler's body touched the ground aside from his feet then he lost. If both fell down at once the last to hit the ground was deemed the winner. If it was unclear which wrestler hit the ground first the fall was disqualified and the match would be started again. A win could also be achieved if either party lost his grip on the other while his opponent still retained his hold. The traditional costume consisted of long johns and an embroidered vest with a velvet centre piece over the top. Matches were usually decided by the best of three falls.[139]

Young Isaac was to find himself once again before the magistrate and in gaol over Christmas in 1849:

> MAGISTRATES' OFFICE, WORKINGTON December. 12. Isaac Cragg, of Cockermouth, waller, pleaded guilty to using obscene and indecent language within the limits of the town of Workington, and was committed to the house of correction, Carlisle, for fourteen days, in default of payment of fine of 10s. and costs.[140]

---

[138] Carlisle Journal - Saturday 24 September 1842

[139] http://en.wikipedia.org/wiki/Cumberland_and_Westmorland_wrestling

[140] Carlisle Journal - Friday 14 December 1849

John's, more decent daughter, Elizabeth, married William Grave on 19 August 1843, and signed with an 'X'.[141] William Grave declared himself as a cordwainer (shoemaker) by trade. William and Elizabeth were living in Pearsons Yard, off Castle Street, in 1851, with no children to account for. Elizabeth was employed as a shoe binder at this time.[142] On the corner of Pearsons Yard and Castle Street lived Elizabeth's first cousin Henry Cragg and his family.

Another daughter Sarah died at 10 years of age and was buried at All Saints on 9 March 1843.

Ruth, who was John and Jane's eldest child, married Henry Hodgson on 6 August 1836. Ruth and Henry's eldest son John Hodgson (born 1836) was 11 years of age when he found himself in some trouble. He was brought before the Epiphany Sessions for the County of Cumberland in the Court House at Carlisle on Tuesday 4 January 1848 with the charge of stealing "9s. 4d., the property of Margaret Ritson, of Dovenby" on Saturday 6 November. Before the Chairman E. W. Hasell, Esq., magistrates and a grand jury, John was defended by Mr Ramshay. Mr Dykes represented the prosecution.

Margaret Ritson was a widow, who owned a shop in Dovenby, which was quite close to the Hodgsons' residence. John frequented the shop and often bought flour from for his mother Ruth there. One Sunday morning the shopkeeper found she was missing half-a-crown, four shillings, and a fourpenny piece after John has visited the day before. Evidently, John was seen later that day going to the Public House and approaching another gentleman by the name of Richard Harris; asking him to come with him to buy some bacon, with the promise of some taffy in exchange for accompanying him. The bacon was never purchased, but John apparently had with him some money he had previously buried in the garden, after his mother Ruth had "taken" his money he had in the house. A police constable apprehended him on the Monday following the alleged theft. At that stage John claimed the money he had on him came from his mother and was to be delivered to his aunt Esther Birkett in Cockermouth. Ruth was called as a witness and stated she gave 8s to John on 1 November to buy some meal from Aunt Esther, which he had intended to do so on Saturday 6 November. Ruth's sister Elizabeth Grave (nee Cragg) was then called a witness.

> I live at Cockermouth, and my husband is a shoemaker. The prisoner came my house about 11 o'clock on the 6th of November, and stopped some time. He got some wax ends to tie on a whip, and then went away, saying was going to his aunt Esther's to buy some meal for his mother. My two brothers went for it with him. When they came back they all got dinner with my father, John Cragg, who lives 18 or 20 yards from our house. At one o'clock, just as the factory bell rung, I saw them outside, playing at

marbles. I asked him if he was not going home. He said he was, and he went. I saw no more of him. Cross-examined—I went into my father's to "late" [seek] him to get his dinner, and found him getting it there, off[*sic*] fried meat and potatoes.[143]

The prosecution, Mr Dykes, naturally replied...

contending that the alibi attempted to be proved was neither more nor less than false swearing on the part of the witnesses for the defence. [144]

Fortunately the jury returned verdict of "not guilty", primarily due to the prosecution's case was based on suspicion rather anything more substantial. Discussion then moved quickly to the Magistrate's concern that the case was brought to this court rather than tried under the Juvenile Offenders Act. The Hodgson family, from Tallentire, married into the Cragg family at least three times in the early to mid-1800s. Elizabeth Hodgson and Solomon Cragg (1832), William Hodgson and Elizabeth Cragg (1833), and Henry Hodgson and Ruth Cragg (1836). All three Cragg's were children of Isaac and Ruth.

John Cragg died in January 1849 within Cockermouth District. There exists a burial record for 14 January 1849 relating to a 56-year-old John Cragg at All Saints, which is only about four years out on his age. His death occurred during the 1848-49 cholera outbreak in Cockermouth.

The timing of his death is supported by the 1851 census, which lists Jane Cragg as the head of the household, relying on parish relief and living in Sand Lane on the corner of Waterloo Street. Solomon and Thomas were still living at home with their mother and employed in "parting thread". This was the same address that Isaac and Ruth Cragg (John's parents) had lived at, up until Ruth's death in 1849. John and his family could have moved in with Ruth and Isaac sometime between 1841 and 1849.

Thomas, the youngest son and thread maker, enlisted in 15th Foot Regiment's 2nd Battalion on 4 August 1858 as it was being raised in Whitehaven, Cumberland. The 2nd Battalion was soon posted to Malta for 4 years and 11 months and then Gibraltar for a further 5 years in 1863. During this time, the Battalion saw no major action. In Gibraltar, after 2 years and 4 months, Private Thomas Cragg (No. 818) was discharged on 28 February 1866 after he was "found unfit for further service" for health reasons and returned to Cumberland county. The 1871 Census located Thomas (now employed as a coal miner) newly living in the town of Washington, Durham county with his wife Susannah and their baby daughter Mary. He had

---

[143] Carlisle Journal - Friday 07 January 1848
[144] Carlisle Journal - Friday 07 January 1848

married Susannah Digney on 15 February 1858 at All Saints Church, Cockermouth just as many of his family had married in the past.

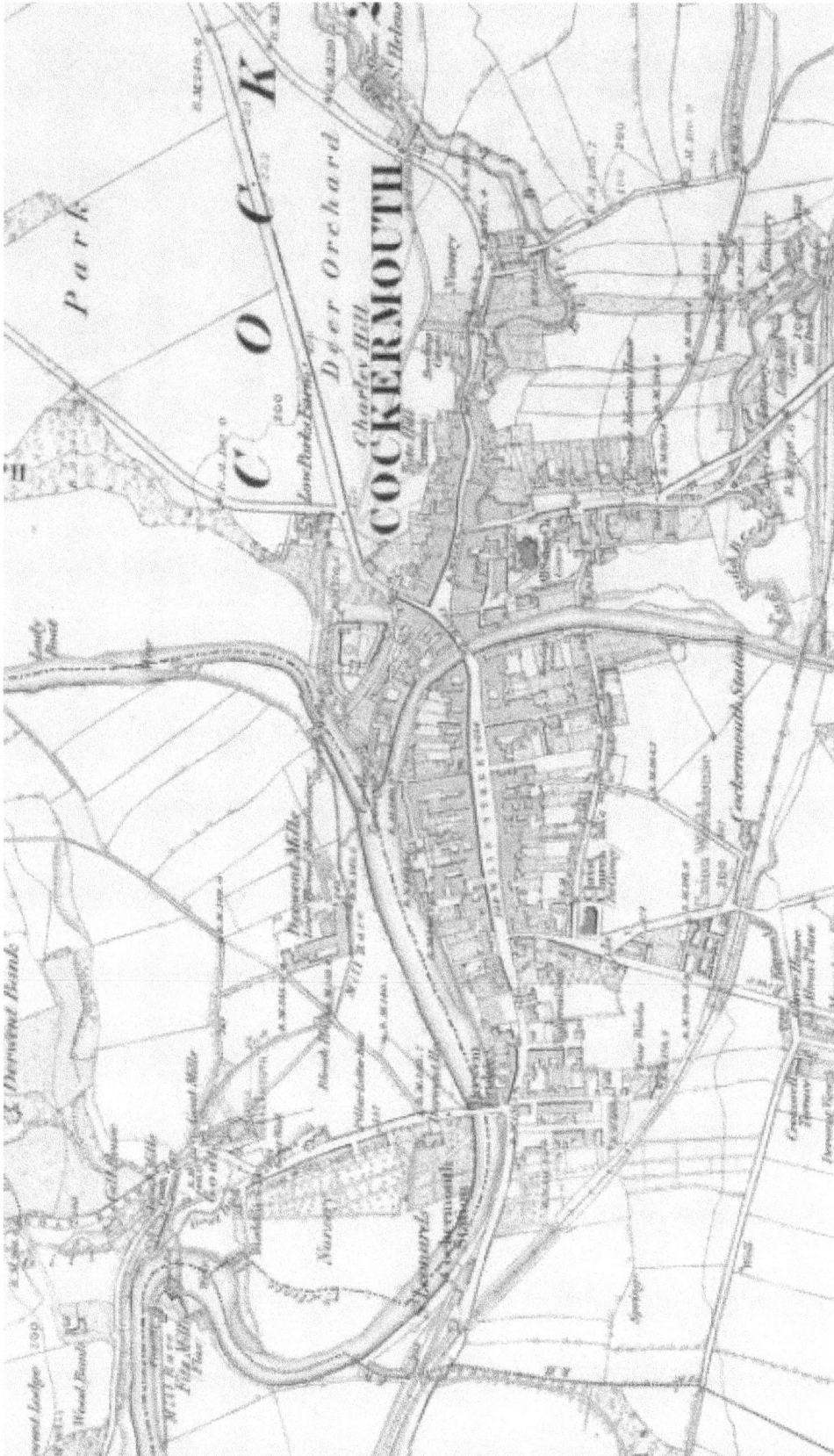

Figure 37 Cockermouth 1864 - Ordnance Survey Cumberland LIV (includes: Brigham; Dean; Greysouthen.) 1867

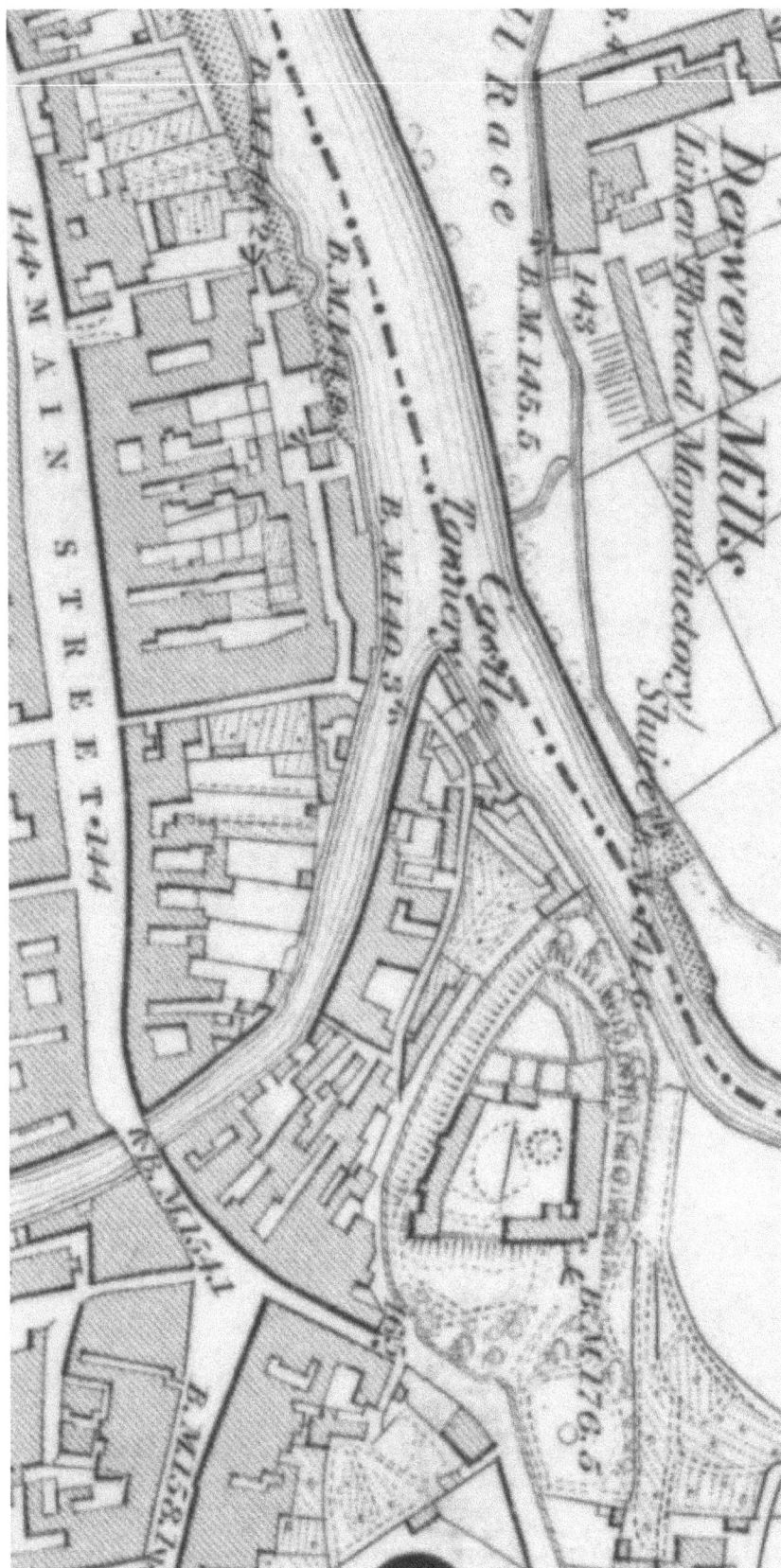

**Figure 38 Cockermouth Castle, Market Lane (High Sand Lane), Brewery Lane and Tanneries
(Ordnance Survey Cumberland LIV (includes: Brigham; Dean; Greysouthen.) 1867)**

Chapter Eight - Joseph Cragg (1803-1878) and Hannah Grave (1803-1878)

Isaac and Ruth's fourth child and second son, Joseph, was born 4 April 1803 in Cockermouth, and christened 29 May that same year. Little is known about Joseph until his marriage to fellow Cockermouth resident, Hannah Grave on 1 December 1823 at All Saints Church. Joseph signed his name on the register. It seems that whilst the boys of Isaac's family were able to at least write, the girls were often deprived of similar education, which may be the reason behind Joseph's sister Ruth simply signing with an 'X' at her marriage in 1821 to John Birkett. This is supported by the fact that the local Free Grammar School was exclusively a boys school.

Hannah gave birth to seven children between 1825 and 1845. In order, they were Isaac, Henry, Joseph, John, William and Robert Hannah. Where they were christened marked a change in church attendance. The children were not christened at All Saints as every other Cragg family member since 1794, but at the Independent Chapel, which was on Main Street and backed onto High Sand Lane (now Waterloo St.). It is not known why Joseph's family changed churches while the remainder of his larger family appears to have remained at All Saints.

Figure 39 The porch and datestone (1719) of the Independent/Congregational Church

The Independent/Congregational Church in Cockermouth was founded in 1651, and was the first one of its denomination in Cumberland. Since the church was not of the Church of England, the minister was not initially permitted to hold services in Cockermouth. These had to be held secretly in a private house outside of the town. Finally, in 1719 a chapel was built in Main Street. In 1850, the present church was built in front of the chapel at a cost of £2,200, and contained enough seating for 500 persons. The latter was used as a Sunday School and Lecture Hall. In 1990, considerable alterations took place, which saw the chapel changed into flats for the mentally handicapped. The church was split into two levels, with the meeting hall above the offices, chapel and kitchen.[145] The porch of the 1719 chapel can still be seen today behind the current United Reformed Church, with the 1719 date stone above the entrance way. At the time of Joseph and Hannah's attendance, Reverend Edward Gatley was a local minister, with a reputation for "earnest piety and intense devotion".

During Joseph and Hannah's time at the Independent/Congregational Church a very strict minister, Rev. Joseph Mather, arrived on the scene, in 1825, and the congregation numbers by 1833 had dropped to 29. Rev. Mather quickly gained a reputation for "his rigid enforcement of the discipline of the Church." In 1869, it was commented that "He would have been a sturdy Puritan two centuries ago, or a good martyr three centuries ago." Fortunately, he only served eight years and less authoritarian ministers arrived on the scene, causing congregation numbers to be built up once again. The new gothic style building was built in front of the old one under Reverend Portas Hewart Davison. It could seat 500 parishioners and cost £2,200 to erect. On the opening day, 11 September 1850, special trains were put on for the 1,600 who attended. That day Rev. Dr Baffles, of Liverpool, preached in the morning from Isaiah xii, 27, and in the evening from Psalm xcv, 7, and Heb. iii, 7.[146]

In 1819, on 25 June a petition from Protestant Dissenters was sent to the House of Lords from Cockermouth requesting the right of the Dissenting ministers to solemnise marriages, rather than conforming to the "Formularies of the Established Church of England".[147] A year later, they presented another petition to the House of Commons requesting universal emancipation in regards to religious worship. Curiously, the petition only supported the rights of Roman Catholics to religious freedom.

Church rates, for All Saints were an expected expense of all householders and renters in Cockermouth, who paid 4d in the pound. In 1834, this was challenged by so-called radicals who consisted of Deists, Dissenters and Republicans, who on principle opposed paying for the church they chose not to attend. The Church Wardens had mistakenly set the rate at 1d that year, believing that sufficient funds had been left over from the previous year. A Vestry meeting was held to resolve the issue and find additional funds to make up the difference. The radical came up with a way to derail the plans of the Church Wardens. They would vote for the rate to be halfpenny in a pound, which would obviously not cover the year's costs, which required 1½d a pound. The group supposedly was composed chiefly of a hundred

---

[145] H. E. Winter, Cockermouth (A History and Guide), 1992.

[146] William Lewis, History of the Congregational church, Cockermouth, 1870

[147] Journals of the House of Lords, Volume 52, 1819.

weavers, a great number of hatters, matchmakers and paupers. One the side of the Church Wardens was Isaac Cragg, tanner, and on the side of the Radicals was dissenter Joseph Cragg, weaver, his son. The Radicals won by 38 votes![148]

The opportunity for leisure time in the Lake Counties was rare compared to today and holidays fewer as well. Sports involving physical strength and skill were popular as well as betting on the events themselves. Wrestling, horseracing, hunting with hounds for otter, hare, foulmart and fox seems to have been popular along with cockfighting. In a town such as Cockermouth, newsrooms and libraries provided more cerebral enlightenment and social interaction away from the inns and alehouses. Occasional theatre performed by locals or travelling entertainers also provided relief from the tedium of work. Inns and alehouses figured largely in Cockermouth with one inn or alehouse for every 106 people in 1829 and accounted for 17.8 percent of businesses in the town. Indoor entertainment included singing, card and dice games, as well as dancing on special occasions.[149]

By 1830, the combination of the industrial revolution and the town's geographic location determined that Cockermouth was to play a pivotal role:

> The town possesses many local advantages of situation, the surrounding country being populous and fertile, having a plentiful supply of water from two fine streams, and three sea ports within a short distance. Its trade comprises the manufacture of woollens, cotton checks, thread, tanned leather, hats, &c. Upon the streams of the Derwent and Cocker are corn and spinning mills, a paper mill, and a carding mill; and about three miles distant, at Greysouthern and Broughton, are extensive coal mines. The views from the high grounds over the country around here are of a pleasing and varied character, embracing clear streams, fertile valleys, and wood-clad hills..." [150]

The 1841 census located Joseph and his family living half way along the southern side of Main Street in Cockermouth, between the Cocker Bridge and Dr Richard Bell's house (on the corner of Sullart Street). Their neighbours were a publican, hatter, tailor (John Simpson), blacksmith (John Steel) and draper (George Sanderson). All the Cragg children were present on the night of the census, except Hannah who was to be born four years later. It was common to encounter large families living in houses though poor health and disease often kept the numbers down. In 1821, Cockermouth had on average 5.3 people living in a house. Often this number would include boarders and other relatives as the average number of people per family was 4.9 and

---

[148] Cumberland Pacquet, and Ware's Whitehaven Advertiser - Tuesday 22 July 1834.

[149] C.M.L Bouch and G.P. Jones, The Lake Counties, 1500-1800 by, 1961, Manchester University Press.

[150] Pigots 1830 Directory.

average number of families per house was 1.1.[151] In 1841, Joseph was a weaver by trade while his eldest son Isaac was a weaver's apprentice at age 16. The second eldest, Henry, was simply described as employed in a woollen mill, at age 14. As wool was in abundance around Cockermouth, the town became a woollen centre second only in production to Kendal, in Cumberland. Later at the baptism of his son, John, in 1855 Joseph referred to himself as a thread maker.

Working life in the mills was pitiful, as the labourers, sometimes young children, worked considerably long hours (12-14 hours a day) in extremely unsafe and unhealthy conditions. A typical mill in Carlisle in 1826 for example had workers starting at six in the morning and finishing work at half past seven in the evening. They would be given one hour for breakfast and one hour for dinner.[152] When George III came to the throne in 1760, woollen manufactories were the chief export of Britain and were to remain so until about 1810 when cotton became dominant.[153] As a result, mills were in abundance all over the country, more so in the new industrial towns built up around the factories.

In 1829 the main industries of Cockermouth were the manufacture of 'cotton checks, ginghams, coarse woollen goods, linen and linen thread, hats, paper etc.; and in the tanning and dressing of leather'. William and Jonathan Harris at Goat Mills and William Stoddart at Cocker Bridge End were cotton, check and gingham manufacturers. Joseph Grave, woollen manufacturer and Joshua Wharton, flax and tow spinners were operating on Sand Lane (Waterloo Street), with William and Jonathan Harris at Goat Mills and Thomas Robinson at Cocker Bridge End. The main corn mill sites at this date were Double Mills, Gote, 'Raby Banks' (Rubbybanks) and 'near Kirkgate' (possibly referring to Little Mill).[154]

There were two classes of jobs employed in woollen cloth manufacture. That of spinner and weaver. Women and children were most usually spinners, while the men took on the more highly regarded role of weaver. Yet by 1830, this had changed, as the spinners were mostly in the factories while weavers generally worked outside in their homes. It was not difficult to learn how to use a handloom. Consequently, many struggling agricultural labourers were attracted to this new industry and being accustomed to low wages, they inadvertently undercut the income of traditional handloom weavers. To add to the handloom weavers' woes the power loom, introduced in the early 1800s, cut down production time and the need for weavers. Fortunately, for some, the power loom was not immediately suitable for woollen cloth manufacture as it had been for cotton. Riots were a natural outcome in the larger towns,

[151] W. Parson and W. White, History, Directory and Gazetteer of the Counties of Cumberland and Westmorland. (Leeds 1829).
[152] E. Hughes, North County Life in the Eighteenth Century, Vol II. 1965, University of Durham, Great Britain
[153] Kenneth O. Morgan(Ed.), The Oxford Illustrated History of Britain, 1991, Oxford University Press.
[154] 2012 *The WaterMills of Cockermouth* http://www.cockermouth.org.uk/watermills2012.pdf, last accessed 11 Aug 2013

as starvation was not a palatable alternative to the life weavers had enjoyed before. When peace in Europe came in 1815, the situation of many Cumberland weavers became much worse. In May 1819, a strike called in Carlisle quickly spread to Cockermouth. The average wage at this time was only five shillings a week.[155] For domestic weavers pride also had as much to do with their struggle. They were not willing to surrender their liberty and enter power-loom factories, to be subject to the iron will of a mill owner and his overseer.[156] Carlisle's representative in Parliament John Curwen MP tabled a petition in Parliament on 24 May 1819:

> I intreat[sic] the attention of the noble lord and the House to the statement I have to make on the part of the Cotton Weavers of the city of Carlisle. The petition is signed by upwards of 1,200 persons. It discloses a state of Suffering which cannot fail of commanding the pity and commiseration of all within and without the walls. They represent, that on working from 14 to 17 hours a day, and that for six days in the week, their earnings do not amount to more than from five to seven shillings, and that many of them can obtain no work whatever. They state their families to be destitute of necessary food and cloathing[sic], and a prey to misery and disease. Afflicting as is the present moment, the future presents no rational hope of amendment. They blame not their employers, — the depreciated state of the Cotton manufacture is the true cause of their sufferings. These industrious, honest, and unfortunate individuals, from their long, patient, and calamitous endurance, are so bent to the earth, so spirit-broken, as to be compelled to petition this House, as a boon, that which bespeaks the extinction of one of the most powerful feelings of the human heart. In despair of obtaining bread at home, they ask you to expatriate them — to convey them to your colonies. In ceasing to be inhabitants of Britain, it will yet be some consolation to promote the interests of the country that gave them birth, — grievous as it must be to sacrifice all ties of kindred and affection, rather than continue to exist on bounty, exhausting the sources of benevolence to preserve a miserable existence.[157]

Amid increasing distress the handloom weavers, operatives and mechanics, marshalled by the radical wool merchant Andrew Green of Bridekirk, petitioned for free trade and the abolition of the Corn Laws between 1828 and 1829.[158] The price of "Corn" (which included wheat, rye and/or other grain) was an important influence on the cost of living of the average citizen in Britain during the early nineteenth century, as wheat or corn used in the baking of

[155] E. Hughes, North County Life in the Eighteenth Century, Vol II. 1965, University of Durham, Great Britian

[156] J.L. and Barbara Hammond, The Town Labourer 1760-1832 (The New Civilisation), 1917, Longman Group Ltd., London.

[157] UK House of Commons, Hansard 24 May 1819 vol 40 cc671-2

[158] http://www.historyofparliamentonline.org/volume/1820-1832/constituencies/cockermouth

bread was the "staff of life." The Corn Laws enforced a very high "protective" tariff against the importation of wheat into England. Thus, the high tariffs on imported wheat imposed by the Corn Laws had the effect of raising the cost of living and increasing the suffering the poor people in England. Consequently, agitation for the repeal of the Corn Laws began in England as early as 1837 with a bill for their repeal introduced in Parliament each year from 1837 onwards until 1847 when they were eventually repealed. [159]

Several townspeople of Cockermouth arranged a petition that was presented to the House of Commons on 7 May 1828:

> A Petition of several Inhabitants of the borough of Cockermouth, was presented, and read; setting forth, That the Petitioners are fully satisfied that Freedom of Trade is greatly for the general good; and praying for the further abolition of those laws which yet remain to impede it; and to urge the entire abandonment of all protecting duties and bounties, which give an undue preference and a gain to one part of the people at the cost of a very disproportionate loss sustained by the whole community. Ordered, That the said Petition do lie upon the Table, and be printed.

Over the previous two months the Protestant Dissenters of Cockermouth had submitted petitions for the emancipation of Roman Catholics and the right for Catholics to hold public office. [160] However the Earl of Lonsdale opposed these petitions and subsequent motions, attracting further anti-Lowther support.

By this time Cockermouth was well known as a pocket borough which was effectively controlled by the Earl of Lonsdale (Lowther family) who owned most of the land in the borough. Sir James Lowther had bought over half the 278 burgages for £58,000 in 1756, and the borough's representation had been controlled since 1802 by his descendant, the Tory 1st Earl of Lonsdale. Prior to this, control of the borough since 1641 had been in the hands of the Earl of Egremont, but Egremont had now been out played by the Lowther family. [161] Voting at the time was not by secret ballot and naturally led to intimidation of the few hundred eligible voters. For an extended period the Returning Officer for the borough and local Bailiff was Reverend Edward Fawcett who had been granted his curacy at All Saints, Cockermouth by the Earl of Lonsdale himself. Typically a Bailiff's term was a year, so quite often certain individuals would serve every alternate year.

---

[159] http://en.wikipedia.org/wiki/United_Kingdom_general_election,_1852, last accessed 15/08/13

[160] Journals of the House of Commons, Volume 83, 1828. H.M. Stationery Office.

[161] The Making of a Pocket Borough: Cockermouth 1722-1756, J. V. Beckett, Journal of British Studies, Vol. 20, No. 1 (Autumn, 1980), pp. 140-157, Cambridge University Press

The 1820 election, held on 10 March, was typical of the undemocratic process which played out in the borough each time. The sitting Members, Lonsdale's nephew John Henry Lowther and his son-in-law, the judge advocate Sir John Beckett were returned unopposed. Beckett, who attended the affair, had dined at the Globe with the bailiff and returning officer, the Rev. Edward Fawcett, rector of Cockermouth, the proposers, the Rev. Henry Lowther, rector of Dissington, Robert Blakeney, collector of customs at Whithaven, the Rev. Richard Armistead, vicar of Cockerham, Lancashire, and 70 others, whilst Lonsdale's Whitehaven colliers had kept order outside.[162] Cockermouth had only one constable at this time, who was powerless to control the mobs.

The 1830 election appeared to be no different except opposition to the undemocratic nature of the process was gaining momentum, especially when supposed secret deals were being made behind the scenes between the Lowthers and other such "borough mongers". This time Lord Lowther and John Henry Lowther deputized for their candidates Philip Pleydell-Bouverie and Randolph Stewart (Viscount Garlies) at the election. Upon encountering an assembly of riotous weavers, they were forced to dispense with the chairing. Joseph Cragg, a politically active weaver at age 26 was likely in the midst of this uproar. In response, the Lowthers and their supporters dined and gathered in force at the county election in the town the following week, when, as expected, the Whigs exposed and denounced the secret deals, but with little effect.[163]

On 5 November 1830, Mr Daniel O'Connell MP from Ireland tabled a petition for the Reform of Parliament on the behalf of Cockermouth which led to much debate. However the focus of debate centered on the intemperate tone and language O'Connell used, rather than the heart of the matter. Fortunately for Cockermouth the petition was ordered to be printed.

> I have to present a petition from certain operatives and mechanics of Cockermouth, extremely well drawn up. It sets forth the present unhappy state of the country; it notices the usurpation, by a few, of the right of representation belonging to the people; thus making this House the properly of a small number, instead of the nation; and attributes to that circumstance undue promotion in the army and navy, the great expense incurred in the collection of the revenue, and the heavy burden of the Church; as also the monopoly of the East India Company, slavery, and the corn-laws; and adds that we cannot expect relief whilst the Legislature is constituted as it now is, and prays for annual Parliaments, universal suffrage, and election by ballot. In the two last

---

[162] Whitehaven Gazette, 13, 20 Mar.; Cumb. Pacquet, 14 Mar. 1820. As cited by Margaret Escott in http://www.historyofparliamentonline.org/volume/1820-1832/constituencies/cockermouth
[163] http://www.historyofparliamentonline.org/volume/1820-1832/constituencies/cockermouth

prayers I concur with the petitioners, and as to voting by ballot in particular. I cannot believe any man to be sincerely desirous of reform who is not a friend of the ballot, for reform consists, first, in every man being enabled to vote as he chooses, which he cannot do without voting by ballot. The petitioners anticipate tremendous danger to the country if the House do not agree to its own reform. I fear, Sir, that their words are prophetic; for the state of the Legislature is now such that any man who gets into favour with the oligarchy, may be Prime Minister, even if he be mad, nay, he may denounce himself as insane and yet be made Minister, and being Minister may prove himself insane, and yet retain his station. Such is our condition, that madmen may be near the helm of the state; and much am I afraid that some are near it now, for if there were not I hardly think the present incompetent and imbecile Administration would have continued to exist so long. I hope the oligarchy will soon see that their safety will be endangered if they continue to entrust their vessel to a pilot who admits he would be out of his senses if he attempted to steer.[164]

On 15 November 1830, yet another petition from Cockermouth was tabled in the House of Commons by Sir James Graham requesting the Reform of Parliament:

I have to present a petition on a subject, which the motion of the Honourable and Learned Member for the county of York will only make the prelude to similar petitions from every city and county in the kingdom—it is from Cockermouth, and prays for the Reform of Parliament. The petitioners state that the inhabitants of the town generally are excluded from any choice of a representative to serve in Parliament; it having been decided by a resolution of the House that the election rested with the burgesses only. —To lie on the Table, and to be printed.[165]

The Reverend Edward Fawcett refused to convene a widely publicized reform meeting for 15 February 1831, as it would have been contrary to Lord Lonsdale's (his patron) wishes. However, it proceeded regardless under the chairmanship of the Rev. John Benson, the vicar of St. Helen's. Pro-reform resolutions were moved by the attorneys Isaac Brown, Joshua Sim, John Steel and John Fisher, and backed by the leading Cumberland Whigs Frecheville, Lawson, Ballatine, Dykes and the Rev. Christopher Wybergh (Vicar of Isel), who vainly objected to the incorporation of the radicals' resolutions adding the ballot, civil list reductions and abolition of the property tax to the petition. The First Lord of the Admiralty, Sir James Graham, presented a petition for reform on 26 February 1831 to the House of Commons.[166]

---

[164] The Mirror of Parliament for the First Session of the Ninth Parliament of Great Britain and Ireland, 1831.

[165] The Mirror of Parliament for the First Session of the Ninth Parliament of Great Britain and Ireland, 1831.

[166] http://www.historyofparliamentonline.org/volume/1820-1832/constituencies/cockermouth, last accessed 16/09/13

Graham delivered another petition 19 March from Cockermouth in support of the Grey ministry's reform bill, by which Cockermouth stood to lose one Member.[167] On 22 March, a second reading of the Reform Bill was held and was carried with 302 voting for and 301 against! Cockermouth's Whig members Viscount Garlies and Bouverie had voted in favour of the Bill. A month later the Tory opposition, most notably Isaac Gascoyne put forward an amendment, which was designed to wreck the Reform Bill. He succeeded with a division of 299-291. Lord Grey responded by requesting the dissolution of Parliament, and at the ensuing general election on 30 April 1831 the reformers were triumphant. Gascoyne himself lost his seat, and of the 34 English county Members who had voted for his amendment, only six survived.[168] Unfortunately, in Cockermouth, both Garlies and Bouverie also lost their seats when the Reverend Edward Fawcett, assisted by the colliery owner Joseph Harris of Greysouthern, the surgeon Samuel Fox of High House, John Steward of Hensingham and William Fell of Cartmel, presided over the return of John Henry Lowther with another anti-reformer, the former attorney-general and Whig turncoat Sir James Scarlett, for whom Lord Lowther deputized. [169] Cockermouth was still in danger of losing one of its two seats and was only saved after a petition to the House of Lords for the inclusion of additional towns (Brigham, Papcastle, Bridekirk, Eaglesfield and a detached part of Dovenby) to the constituency succeeded, giving it a total population of 6,002 and an estimated 356 £10 voters.[170]

The eventual Reform Act of 1832, passed in December 1831, extended the right to vote beyond the burgesses in Cockermouth. In county constituencies, in addition to forty-shilling freeholders, franchise rights were extended to owners of land in copyhold worth £10 (£8000 in 2007) and holders of long-term leases (more than sixty years) on land worth £10 and holders of medium-term leases (between twenty and sixty years) on land worth £50 and to tenants-at-will paying an annual rent of £50. In borough constituencies, such as Cockermouth, all male householders living in properties worth at least £10 a year were given the right to vote – a measure which introduced to all boroughs a standardised form of franchise for the first time. Existing borough electors retained a lifetime right to vote, however they only qualified provided they were resident in the boroughs in which they were electors. In those boroughs which had freemen electors; voting rights were to be enjoyed by future freemen as well, provided their freeman-ship was acquired through birth or apprenticeship and they too were a resident. Returns submitted in January 1832 by Wood and Fawcett noted 1,002 houses in the current constituency, substituted an assessed tax valuation of £608 18s. 7d. for the £540

---

[167] House of Commons, Debates 19 March 1831 vol 3 cc578-9,

http://hansard.millbanksystems.com/commons/1831/mar/19/minutes#S3V0003P0_18310319_HOC_2, last accessed 16/09/13.

[168] Terry Jenkins, http://www.histparl.ac.uk/gascoynes-wrecking-amendment-1831, last accessed 17/9/13

[169] http://www.historyofparliamentonline.org/volume/1820-1832/constituencies/cockermouth, last accessed 16/09/13

[170] http://www.historyofparliamentonline.org/volume/1820-1832/constituencies/cockermouth, last accessed 16/09/13

previously supposed, and stipulated that rack rent adjustment alone would increase the number of £10 houses in Cockermouth from 235 to over 300. [171]

The Reform Act of 1832 gave 1 in 7 men in the United Kingdom the right to vote.[172] Those who did not receive that right were known as "non-electors". Some of these non-electors sought to the influence the politicians of the day through other means, especially when there was talk of introducing a bread tax which brought to mind the old corn laws which had only been repealed five years prior. In the 1832 West Cumberland election the so-called independent Returning Officer had the Cockermouth hustings held in the Castle-Yard at a cost of £26.[173]

By the late 1830s, McCulloch noted that 'A good many particulars ... have changed within the last 30 years. No domestic manufactures are now carried on...', which implied trades such as domestic weaving had finally succumbed to the Mills.[174] Thus, the spinning and weaving of wool, cotton and flax were now largely carried out in factories. Due to geography, these mills were on the fringes of the Lake District, at Stevely, Kendal, Ulverston and Cockermouth. The mills became the centre of communities, with terraced housing for workers situated close by. Many examples have been largely preserved in Cockermouth.

The predicament of the poor handloom weavers was notorious in the 1830s, and their situation continued to deteriorate. A parliamentary select committee produced reports on petitions from the weavers in 1834 and 1835. It was chaired by Sir John Maxwell, 7th Baronet, who with John Fielden called witnesses sympathetic to the weavers. Fielden via Maxwell introduced a minimum wage bill in parliament in 1835. The opposition of *laisse faire* members meant it had no chance; but Fielden continued to advocate action.

On 19 February 1839, another petition was presented to the House of Commons from Cockermouth requesting the repeal of the Corn Laws. It was one of many petitions presented in that sitting and numerous were also presented in favour of the laws. One petition from Manchester stated:

> These petitioners, the hand-loom weavers of Manchester, state, that although they are compelled to work fourteen or fifteen hours a-day, they are unable to obtain even the necessaries of life; that they are totally destitute of furniture and of beds; that they have no means of educating their children; and they further say, that they fear there will be no remedy for the severe distress they are now suffering, unless foreign corn be

---

[171] http://www.historyofparliamentonline.org/volume/1820-1832/constituencies/cockermouth, last accessed 16/09/13

[172] http://en.wikipedia.org/wiki/Reform_Act_1832, last accessed 15/08/13

[173] Return of Number of Electors enrolled on Registers in each County, City and Borough in Great Britain, 1833, HOUSE OF COMMONS PAPERS; ACCOUNTS AND PAPERS, Paper Number: (189) Volume/page: XXVII.21

[174] J. R. McCulloch, Statistical Account of the British Empire (London, 1837) Volume 1.

allowed to be imported free of duty. They pray your Honourable House to take their statements into consideration, and allow evidence to be heard at the bar.[175]

The vote to repeal the laws was defeated with 172 for and 161 against. The two local Whig MP's at the time, Henry Aglionby and Edward Horsman had voted in favour of the repeal.

It is not conclusively known, whether the Cragg family members, who were handloom weavers, actually entered the mills or worked domestically. Only when the weavers were facing starvation did they consider sending their children into the mills.[176] Joseph sent his son Henry into a mill for work before the age of 14, but the other sons John and Joseph aged 12 and 10 were not employed in a mill in 1841. This suggests that the situation for Joseph and his family was not as drastic as for those families in the large industrial towns, such as Carlisle. However, the family would have certainly appreciated the extra income brought home by Henry. It could also suggest employment in the mills was difficult to come by. In 1841 according to the reports submitted by Inspectors of Factories to Parliament in June, it was the case that many mills (including those in Cockermouth) were suffering from a "stagnation of trade" and only operating four days a week, whilst others had stopped trading altogether. Equipment from failed mills was broken up as scrap after being sold for 90% below its original value. Wages had dropped, primarily due to the shorter hours, from a guinea (approx. 21s) to 14s a week. Men of 18 and 20 years of age were willing to accept roles normally reserved for children such as piecers for 6s to 7s a week.[177] Piecers had to lean over the spinning-machine to repair the broken threads.

The Royal Commission on Hand-Loom Weavers, eventually set up in 1837, was an enquiry into unemployment and poverty in the textile industry. Nassau William Senior chaired the Royal Commission. With him on the control board were William Edward Hickson, J. Leslie, and Samuel Jones-Loyd. A number of reports were issued between 1837 and 1841. The fact-finding carried out by the assistant commissioners in 1837–8 occurred against a background of widespread unrest. By 1840, the number of weavers had dropped by 100,000. Many weavers, in significant numbers, had become Chartists of the "physical force" tendency.

The stipulated the six main aims of the Chartist movement as published in 1838 were:

1. A vote for every man twenty-one years of age, of sound mind, and not undergoing punishment for crime.

---

[175] Barrow, John, *The Mirror of Parliament for the Second Session of the Fourteenth Parliament of Great Britain and Ireland*, Volume 1, 1839.

[176] J.L. and Barbara Hammond, The Town Labourer 1760-1832 (The New Civilisation), 1917, Longman Group Ltd., London.

[177] REPORT by Leonard Homer, Esq., Inspector of Factories, for the Quarter ending the 30th of June, 1841.House of Commons Papers, Volume 6, Great Britain. Parliament. House of Commons, H.M. Stationery Office, 1841

2. The secret ballot. - To protect the elector in the exercise of his vote.

3. No property qualification for members of Parliament - thus enabling the constituencies to return the man of their choice, be he rich or poor.

4. Payment of members, thus enabling an honest tradesman, working man, or other person, to serve a constituency, when taken from his business to attend to the interests of the Country.

5. Equal Constituencies, securing the same amount of representation for the same number of electors, instead of allowing small constituencies to swamp the votes of large ones.

6. Annual parliaments, thus presenting the most effectual check to bribery and intimidation, since though a constituency might be bought once in seven years (even with the ballot), no purse could buy a constituency (under a system of universal suffrage) in each ensuing twelve-month; and since members, when elected for a year only, would not be able to defy and betray their constituents as now.

In April 1839, in a communication to the Home Secretary, Lord John Russell, the magistrates of Cockermouth stated that as a consequence of the violent conduct by the Chartists, and the knowledge that a considerable number of pikes had been made, and were still being made in Cockermouth and the adjoining villages and "language was held out of a general rising"; that the magistrates really did not know how to act. The magistrates asked for a company of infantry to be stationed in Cockermouth, which had no police. They feared that life and property would soon "be in an insecure state".

> That a considerable number of pikes had been made, and are still making, in this town (Cockermouth), and in the towns and villages in this neighbourhood. That they are made as ordered, and paid for when taken away. The makers of these weapons are well known. That the language of the Chartists is highly seditious and violent; that they hold out that they are to have a general rising, &c. That the magistrates, by the existing laws, have no power to keep any arms seized, or of detaining them from the parties, to whom they must be returned. That, therefore, the magistrates are compelled to solicit advice from her Majesty's Government with respect to a search for arms in the first place, and, also, in case of the expected meeting (which, it is apprehended, is for the purpose of drilling), such instructions as may exonerate them hereafter from being charged with supineness and neglect of duty on the one hand, or of illegal rashness on the other. The magistrates also solicit your Lordship that a company of infantry may be quartered in Cockermouth whilst the present state of things continues.[178]

---

[178] John Henry Barrow, The Mirror of Parliament, Volume 6, House of Commons, Monday 29 July 1839.

Russell refused to respond or act. As a result, the anxiety of the inhabitants had greatly increased, and, at a meeting at which all the magistrates attended, they unanimously resolved to put themselves under the direction of any person the Government might select. An application was made to the Government for arms, which were peremptorily refused. In the meantime, from the excited state of the town, and there being no troops within twenty-six miles, it was deemed expedient by the magistrates to send for the militia staff from Whitehaven, consisting of eight men, as a nucleus round which they might rally. Russell roundly criticized the magistrates for incurring unnecessary expenses in bringing the militia to Cockermouth and claimed he had not received any other communication on the matter.

Russell went on to later remark:

> ".. that on former occasions, whenever there is a political movement, either for good or evil in any part of her Majesty's dominions, that movement is sure to extend itself to the patriotic town of Cockermouth, where radicals and ragmen have so large a share of influence with a certain portion of its inhabitants"[179].

The agitation was to be further inflamed on Wednesday 22 May 1839. In the midst of much excitement in Cockermouth, Chartists formed a procession and preceded by banners and music, marched for Aspatia to join a gathering of other chartists from Wigton, Carlisle, Dalston and Maryport Once there, the crowd was addressed by a number of passionate orators and after which they returned to their respective towns again heralded by banners and music. *The Cumberland Pacquet* judged the affair to be a failure, but obviously had no sympathy for the Chartist cause.

On the following day, the political agitator George Julian Hearney arrived in Cockermouth on the Carlisle coach,

> ...the town presently became a scene of agitation, and bustle and importance everywhere manifested itself. Anxiety prevailed to a considerable extent on the part the respectable inhabitants for their personal security and the tranquillity of the town, whilst all was animation and excitement on the part of the Chartists in convening preparatory meetings and arranging their plans for holding one upon a more extensive scale in the evening. Prior to the meeting taking place, it appears that two associations were formed, namely, "A Female Chartist Association." and "An Infant Chartist Association."[180]

---

[179] *Cumberland Pacquet, and Ware's Whitehaven Advertiser* - Tuesday 28 May 1839
[180] *Cumberland Pacquet, and Ware's Whitehaven Advertiser* - Tuesday 28 May 1839

A request was drawn up for a major public gathering to be held later that evening and presented to the local magistrate Rev. Edward Fawcett. The requisition was

> We, the undersigned householders of the borough of Cockermouth, request your permission to hold a public meeting in the market place, on Thursday the 23d May, at eight o'clock the evening, for the purpose of giving explanation of the principles of the people's charter : John Peill. John Fearon. John Elliot. Joseph Green. Rodger Mather. Robert McAdam. John Fisher, jun. Joseph Wilkinson."[181]

Fawcett obviously wanted nothing to do with the request, which in his mind encouraged inflammatory and revolutionary ideas. The Chartists proceeded regardless.

> The meeting; was nevertheless held in the old Market Place, at eight o'clock in the evening, where about four hundred men, women, and children were gathered together. As matter of course, George Julian Hearney was the star of the evening. This worthy, as well three or four others, addressed the assembly from butcher's stall, in language the most seditious and disgraceful. The outpourings, however, of the rebellious Hearney far outstripped those of all his inflammatory colleagues, and were of such incendiary and diabolical nature as to be utterly unfit for the public eye. Suffice it to say, however, that in terms the most seditious and inflammatory, he recommended physical force, burning, robbery, and bloodshed !!! told the Chartists that June would be "sacred month"—no work to be done after its commencement— every one was to live by plunder—and to work no more till put in possession of their political rights! Such is the "explanation of the principles of the people's Charter"[182]

Political thought in Cockermouth did not always align with the *Cumberland Pacquet*, but the majority of the men in Cockermouth were less radical in nature and confined themselves to supporting the Whig and Tory parties and their local representatives. There was sympathy for the weavers who had to "toil long hours in unwholesome apartments without being able to earn wherewith to purchase the necessaries of life for themselves and families". However, less revolutionary and more civilised means were encouraged to achieve reform and the ultimately the lifting of financial hardship.

---

[181] *Cumberland Pacquet, and Ware's Whitehaven Advertiser* - Tuesday 28 May 1839
[182] *Cumberland Pacquet, and Ware's Whitehaven Advertiser* - Tuesday 28 May 1839

In June 1839, the Chartists presented a large petition to the House of Commons, but a large majority voted not to even hear what they had to say. With the petition rebuffed, many Chartist leaders advocated widespread use of force (strikes and physical violence) as the only means of attaining their aims. During the Chartist disturbances a detachment of Metropolitan policemen were sent to a number of towns including Cockermouth.[183]

COCKERMOUTH. CHARTIST DEMONSTRATIONS. The recent events at Birmingham have set the Chartists everywhere on the move, and they are threatening much in future. whatever they may be able to perform. Meetings have held in nearly all the towns in which any number of these misguided men are known to exist, and delegates have been travelling from town to town, haranguing these assemblages in language little calculated to allay their excitement. At Cockermouth on the evening of yesterday week the Chartists mustered their forces, and were addressed at considerable length by Lowry, of Newcastle, the noted Chartist delegate ; since which time they have been on the qui vive, as if preparing for some important event They even carried their daring far on Thursday last as to be openly seen sharpening pikes, and carrying them publicly about the streets! One of these looking weapons is at present in our possession. It is a destructive looking implement, rudely formed iron or steel, about twenty inches long, with a socket at the end in which to fix a poll or shaft. The blade is about an inch broad, thirteen inches from the shoulder to the end, and the length of the socket six inches. There is a cross at the shoulder of the blade, the extreme of which is about eight inches. It is in the form of crescent, both sides, and pointed. One-half the blade is also sharp on both sides, and pointed at the end; the other half nearly a quarter inch thick…It was purchased Cockermouth, a few days ago, by the gentleman who sent it to us, and is of the same size and description as those generally in possession of the Chartists in that town. It is also known as fact in Cockermouth that the females who are members of the Female Chartists' Association," are so wretchedly infatuated as also to have armed themselves. Their weapons of offence are small daggers, about eight inches long, sharp-pointed, and barbed on both sides, which they are enabled to conceal about their persons. In consequence of these demonstrations the neighbouring Magistrates held a meeting at Cockermouth on Tuesday last at which nearly the whole of the respectable inhabitants were sworn in special constables, and an express was sent off to Carlisle for the military. Friday evening fifty privates, three sergeants, and a trumpeter, commanded by two officers, namely, Captain Currie and Ensign Bingham, marched into the town, and took up their

---

[183] Frederick Clare Mather, Public Order in the Age of the Chartists, Manchester University Press, 1959

quarters at the Globe, the Huntsman, and the Apple Tree inns, to the no small joy of the peaceable inhabitants, and the terror and discomfiture of the Chartists, who have since remained in quietness.[184]

A sailor (midshipman) who had spent 19 July 1839 in Cockermouth recalled:

The Chartists had constantly been assembling in formidable parties, and much anxiety was prevailing in the town: night after night the crisis was expected, and the town was to be fired. The magistrates had taken it in turn to sit up all the night through, and were now sitting at the "Globe," where I had taken up my quarters, and where I soon learnt that a detachment of soldiers had likewise taken theirs. Two post-chaises had just arrived with some of the metropolitan police, who evidently created a little sensation. I candidly admit I wished myself any where else than at Cockermouth.[185]

The authorities soon intervened and rounded up the chief protagonists of violence. Apprehended on Sunday 7 July on charges of sedition, Harney was taken to Warwick Gaol and tried at the Birmingham Assizes. As a result, a planned general strike for 12 August was called off and Harney went into exile for a year after the jury refused to indict him. He returned a year later and organised general strikes in 1842, which earned him another court trial at Lancaster, with 57 other Chartists.

In the Cumberland Quarter Sessions held in late 1839 it was revealed in a case presided over by Rev. Edward Fawcett how much influence the Chartist movement had held in Cockermouth. It was known that an affiliated society had existed in the town, but now it was revealed how many dangerous weapons (pikes and daggers) had been manufactured locally to carry out the objectives of the society as advocated by the "physical force" chartists.

In the town, it was known, that there were upwards of 300 pikes of the most formidable description, which had been made for the purpose of breaking the peace and disturbing the order and quiet of the country.[186]

As part of the Royal Commission in 1840, the assistant commissioner Richard Muggeridge reported on the state of Hand Loom Weavers in Lancashire, Westmorland, Cumberland, and part of the West Riding of Yorkshire with a further report on Ireland. In the commission's final report dated 19 February 1841, Muggeridge noted that:

---

[184] Cumberland Pacquet, and Ware's Whitehaven Advertiser - Tuesday 16 July 1839

[185] Letter to The Editor by "A Midday ashore" *Rambles at Home*, The Nautical Magazine, 1840,

[186] Cumberland Quarter Sessions, The Champion (London, United Kingdom), October 27, 1839, Issue 163, p.2

The Cockermouth average [weekly wage] was for the cotton, or check and gingham weaving 7s. 5½d weekly, when fully employed. On 353 looms so engaged. 216 were worked by adult males, 59 by boys and 34 by women and girls; 41 were standing idle. The weavers of Cockermouth are mostly engaged in weaving shops or factories, which will explain their comparatively high wage earnings. Of the boys and girls, about 3 out of 5 were the children of the weavers.[187]

He found that the alleged causes of the depressed conditions the Northern handloom weavers were experiencing were:

1. The influence and operation of the present laws affecting and regulating the importation of foreign grain.
2. The competition of power looms.
3. The abatements made by employers, from the wages of the weavers; and the inefficiency of the present arbitration act.
4. The competition among the masters
5. The disproportionate number of weavers, to the labour required to be performed by them.
6. The fact of a knowledge of the weaving trade being easily acquired, and of the trade itself, being open to all classes of unemployed persons.
7. Foreign competition
8. The exportation of yarn and machinery.

By 1841, the situation for handloom weavers in and around Carlisle had become desperate indeed. In response in December of that year the Council of Carlisle sent a petition to the House of Commons claiming that there were *'nearly 6000 whose average weekly earnings amounted to no more than 1s/2d, comprising more than one quarter of the whole population of the borough...of these the greatest number were handloom weavers'*, some 572 families. Further petitions from Cumberland handloom weavers, the mayor of Carlisle and cotton firms were dispatched to Sir Robert Peel in 1842, 1843 and 1845, protesting trade restrictions and the Corn Laws. The hand loom weaver's petition of May 1842 in particular cited a 50% reduction on wages over the previous 3 years resulting in the average weekly earnings of a handloom weaver to be 3s/-. It was also stated that one sixth of Carlisle's population was engaged in weaving.[188]

---

[187] Hand-loom weavers. Reports from Assistant Hand-Loom Weavers' Commissioners. Part V. Report by W. A. Miles, Esq. on the west of England and Wales. Report by R. M. Muggeridge, Esq. on the counties of Lancaster, Westmorland, Cumberland, and part of the West Riding of Yorkshire. Note to the report of J. C. Symons, Esq., on the south of Scotland., 1840. MILES, William Augustus

[188] E. Hughes, North County Life in the Eighteenth Century, Vol II. 1965, University of Durham, Great Britian

Due to the hardship experienced in the town and surrounding area, the Cockermouth Union Workhouse was built in 1840-1843 on Sullart Street, at a cost of about £4,000. [189] In response to the hardship faced by workers, in 1841 various men of Cockermouth banded together and formed a fraternal lodge in the town under the banner of the United Ancient Order of Druids. The lodge was called *No. 195, Rose of Derwent Vale Lodge* and met at the Greyhound Inn in Cockermouth every alternate Tuesday. The founders were Aaron Jarden, John Bell, John Smith, John Thursby, James Thursby, Isaac Thomlinson, Benjamin Nicolson, William Alpin, William Blackader, George Weight, John Wilkinson, Thomas Wilson and James Reed.[190] The United Ancient Order of Druids were a democratic and socially-conscientious organisation, which was run by an elected Board of Directors with the aim of "social and intellectual intercourse" and "general philanthropy and benevolence"[191] It was not religious organisation, however the members were expected to "preserve and practice the main principles attributed to the early Druids, particularly those of justice, benevolence and friendship."

One of the first activities of the lodge in Cockermouth was to hold a procession through the streets of the town on 1 June 1841.

> Rose of Derwent Vale Lodge, No. *195*, Cockermouth. —The Brothers of this Lodge held their first annual procession on Whit-Tuesday. Early in the day a splendid new banner by Br. Fleming, was hoisted from one of the windows of the Lodge Room, and then began such a joyful scene of activity as was never before witnessed on any similar occasion in Cockermouth. The procession formed about half-past ten, and proceeded to church, where an excellent sermon was preached by the Rev. E. Fawcett. At the conclusion of divine service, a carriage was in waiting, decorated with oak, mistletoe and evergreens, and drawn by spirited horses, into which the Arch Druid with a harp, accompanied by his two Bards entered; the V. A on a bay-horse, and his two Bards on white steeds went next in order, and they were followed by the Brothers in crimson scarfs and white gloves. The procession, headed by an excellent band of music, and several Members bearing flags, banners and wands, paraded the principal streets of the town. On their return to the Lodge Room a sumptuous dinner was served up, of which upwards of one hundred Brethren and friends partook. The evening was spent with much hilarity. Many appropriate speeches, songs, toasts, and sentiments were given, and the company did not separate until a late hour, when all departed highly delighted with the day and evening's amusements. Upon the whole it was such a day

[189] *Askew, John. 1866 A guide to the interesting places in and around Cockermouth*

[190] The Quarterly Magazine and Literary Journal of the United Ancient Order of Druids, 1841, Volume 1 pg 277

[191] Constitutional Laws of the United Ancient Order of Druids (1846). London

as the oldest inhabitant had never seen before, and will make a lasting impression on all parties concerned.[192]

Though, not a recognised founder of the lodge Joseph Cragg was likely part of this scene. Four years later in April 1845, the *Carlisle Journal* reported on his involvement:

> On Monday week, the members the Rose of Derwent Vale Lodge the ancient order of Druids, celebrated the fifth anniversary of their institution by publicly dining together at the house of Mr. Musgrave Todd, the sign of the Crown and Mitre, in Cockermouth. About fifty members, with their friends, sat down to an excellent dinner, served up in a style of uncommon neatness. Mr. James Bolton presided on the occasion, and Mr. Joseph Cragg officiated as vice-chairman. On the cloth being withdrawn, the health of the Queen was proposed as a toast, and received with a burst of enthusiasm worthy of the characteristic loyalty by which the ancient order of Druids is distinguished. Many other loyal and constitutional toasts followed interspersed with songs and recitations, and at ten o'clock the meeting broke up, every member being highly delighted with the agreeable nature of the evening's entertainment, and no less gratified to learn that the affairs of the Lodge are in very prosperous condition.[193]

The Odd Fellows Cocker Lodge was opened in 1857 and provided similar social support to those in need. Ten years earlier, in 1847, the friendly and benefit societies in the town consisted of two lodges of Odd Fellows, a lodge of Forresters, a lodge of Druids, one of Rechabites, and one of Mechanics.

The Mechanic's Institute, established in 1845 by subscription, occupied two large rooms behind the Savings Bank. The late Robert Benson, of St. Helen's, a promoter of the scheme, was the institution's President until his death in 1859. The Library was both extensive and valuable, numbering more than 2,000 volumes. In 1858, it received a magnificent bequest from the late General Benson, of Haseness, in Buttermere, consisting of his whole valuable Library, exceeding 1,000 volumes, together with a legacy of £100. The Reading Room provided the opportunity to peruse the Metropolitan and Provincial Newspapers, and Periodicals. This area of town also contained a House of Correction, and Police Station, which were erected 1854-1856.[194]

The Temperance movement, which featured so prominently in the life of Joseph's son Henry and grandson Joseph Henry, gained a significant foothold in Cockermouth. John Askew, a

---

[192] The Quarterly Magazine and Literary Journal of the United Ancient Order of Druids, 1841, Volume 1 pg 45

[193] Carlisle Journal - Saturday 05 April 1845

[194] *Askew, John. 1866 A guide to the interesting places in and around Cockermouth*

Cockermouth local, who had recently returned from Australia, described how on 17 June 1857 at nearby Pardshaw Crag the friends of temperance held a monster picnic. An estimated 14,000 people attended, joining the throng after travelling in gigs, open carriages and even the humble donkey cart. At the foot of the Crags stood a gaily-decorated marquee that could house up to 3,000 people. Neale Dow, an American temperance promoter spoke to the crowd. However the scene soon resembled a fair, with tumblers, shows, a photographer and cheap knick-knacks on sale. The thirst of the participants knew no bounds however. The local Bee Hive Inn, drained of every drop of intoxicating refreshment, had to send away to Cockermouth for more supplies![195] Amongst the crowd, the Cragg family would have certainly fitted in. A year later, a procession of Rechabites, Good Templars, and Bands of Hope walked from Cockermouth to the Eaglesfield Quaker Meeting House, where 400 indulged in tea.

In the Court House Buildings, the first door on the right led to the Gentlemen's News Room, the subscription was set at the uniform rate of one guinea per annum. The Savings Bank erected in 1846; was a neat building surmounted by the Town's Clock, adjoined the Court House.[196]

The Cockermouth and Workington Railway was opened for traffic and passengers in April 1847 after an Act of Parliament was passed in 1845.[197] The single track was deemed to be a ¾ coal traffic line and ran for 8 ½ miles to Workington Harbour delivering primarily coal from the pits of West Cumberland.[198]

---

[195] *Askew, John. 1866 A guide to the interesting places in and around Cockermouth*

[196] *Askew, John. 1866 A guide to the interesting places in and around Cockermouth*

[197] *Askew, John. 1866 A guide to the interesting places in and around Cockermouth*

[198] Bradshaw's General Railway Directory, Shareholders' Guide, Manual and Almanack, 1857

Figure 40 Hand Loom Weaver 1888

The 1851 census gives a greater insight into the family and their occupations. Joseph and Hannah at 48 years of age were now living in Brewery Lane, with their children John, Robert and Hannah. The description of Joseph's occupation is more detailed stating he was engaged in 'hand loom weaver woollery'. John at age 18 was a tailor's apprentice and Robert 16 was a shoemakers apprentice. Both Henry and Joseph had left home and married by this stage, but there is uncertainty surrounding Isaac's movements after 1841. He is picked up again in 1881, but this will be discussed later. Unfortunately one of the twins William died and was buried in Cockermouth on 22 May 1849 aged 11, by Rev. William Earee who worked at All Saints Church as a curate.

In mid-1852, the borough of Cockermouth was in the midst of a tightly contested election for seats in Parliament. The borough was at that time entitled to have two sitting members, who were Henry Aglionby and Edward Horsman, both of whom were still members of the Whig party. Challenging these two members of parliament was the Conservative General Henry Wyndham, a veteran of the Battle of Waterloo and resident of Cockermouth Castle.

The last Earl, George O'Brien Wyndham, had built a handsome residence adjoining the Castle entrance gateway. His eldest son, Henry Wyndham, continued this work and erected most of the other new buildings within the castle area, and further beautified the surrounding grounds with walks and gardens. [199]

---

[199] *Askew, John. 1866 A guide to the interesting places in and around Cockermouth*

Figure 41 General Henry Wyndham (George Clint, after Thomas Goff Lupton)

The Prime Minister of the day was Lord Derby of the Conservative party who lead a minority Protectionist government. Mostly due to the repeal of the unpopular Corn Laws in 1847, England was now enjoying a period of prosperity. By 1852, the Tory/Conservative party had effectively split into Peelites (after Robert Peel), Free Traders and Tories. The two former groups supported the lifting of trade tariffs and often sided with the Whigs on international trade issues. As a result, the July 1852 United Kingdom general election was a defining moment in the formation of the modern political parties of Britain. Following 1852, the Tory/Conservative party became, more completely, the party of the rural aristocracy, while the Whig/Liberal party became the party of the rising urban bourgeoisie in Britain.[200]

Out of the population of 7,275 in the borough of Cockermouth, only 355 men were registered electors or constituents. Eligibility was granted only to "£10 householders" or "old burgage tenants".[201]

On 5 April 1852 a deputation of non-electors (including Joseph Cragg and two of his sons Henry and Joseph Jr) was received by the Whig representatives Henry Aglionby and Edward Horsman in Cockermouth at the Sun Inn, which stood at the corner of Main Street and Market Street.

---

[200] http://en.wikipedia.org/wiki/United_Kingdom_general_election,_1852, last accessed 15/08/13

[201] Adams's Parliamentary Handbook: A Key to the Houses of Lords and Commons 1854, http://books.google.com.au/books?id=f-YNAAAAQAAJ&dq=General%20Henry%20Wyndham%20castle&pg=PA144#v=onepage&q=General%20Henry%20Wyndham%20castle&f=false, last accessed 16/08/13

Figure 42 Edward Horsman c1876

The canvassing by both sides was renewed that Monday, the market day. In the evening, the Non-Electors of the borough, who appeared to take a lively interest in the contest, went in procession through the streets of the town, accompanied by a band, banners, and by symbolical representations of the small, taxed loaf of bread, and the large, untaxed loaf bread—the small, taxed sugar loaf, and the large, untaxed sugar loaf, which were borne upon stout poles. After they had walked through the streets, they assembled in great force in front of the Sun Inn. Large in numbers and enthusiasm. About half-past six a deputation of non-electors, headed Mr. Archibald Brown, weaver, waited upon Aglionby and Horsman, and presented to them the following address :-

> *To Henry Aglionby Aglionby, Esq-, and Edward Horsman Esq-, the respected Members for the Borough of Cockermouth.* "Gentlemen,—We, the Working Men of the Borough of Cockermouth. beg most respectfully to convey to you through this medium our high sense of the many obligations you have laid us under, thus to give expression to our sentiments and feelings, and to pay you the well-earned tribute your general parliamentary conduct merits at our hands.
>
> That you have uniformly acted up to those principles you have always avowed, no one can have the hardihood deny; and think ourselves justified in believing that the carrying out of those principles admirably illustrates the motto—" The greatest amount happiness to the greatest numbers " And we regard the high position you have taken as indicative of what may confidently anticipate in the future. We might call your attention many and important topics now agitating the nation Its length and breadth—topics which are as familiar to you as "household words," and which need not now reiterate; suffice it to say we are of opinion that no government can ever successfully rule the destinies of this great nation which is not progressive. To attempt such a project as a re-imposition of the Bread Tax—to invert a policy so notoriously successful, and to interrupt a course of such manifest prosperity—can no more be the duty of political party, howsoever designated or composed, than to submerge again the drained fens of Lincolnshire, or to fill up the Bridgewater Canal. How many millions of mouths have been filled with bread for the first time the effects of Free

Trade we shall not attempt to calculate; but the number is large enough to forbid any possibility of a return to artificial restriction. "In conclusion we beg to congratulate you on the success of your canvass, and to convey to you our best assurances that all and every means in our power shall be brought into requisition to place you again in the proud position to which you so deservedly aspire. With our best wishes and endeavours for the accomplishment of your triumphant return to Parliament as members for the Borough of Cockermouth. " We are, gentlemen, for ourselves and on behalf of our fellow workmen, your obedient humble servants. —Leonard Bowe, Archibald Brown, John Barton, Joseph Shearman, Thomas Thursby, William Lamonby. Joseph Cragg, sen., George Fleming. John Thursby, Henry Cragg, John Smith, James Thursby, Joseph Cragg, jun., John Smith, jun., Joseph Meals, John Cattiman, Joseph Johnston, William Gray, Isaac Wilkinson, Henry Wilkin, John Linton, John Braithwaite, John Denwood, James Wilkinson, William Wilkinson, Walter Bowe, William Swain, George Bowman, James Clark, Isaac Barnes." [202]

Henry Aglionby MP and Edward Horsman MP then responded.

Mr.Aglionby then addressed the deputation. He begged they would make allowance for the feelings under which be now addressed them. It would be vain to attempt to give expression in words to the feelings of pride and gratification with which he received this mark their approbation. He had represented Cockermouth for twenty years, and the nonelectors of the borough now assured him that they approved of his conduct. (" Most decidedly.") There could be no greater stimulus to a continuance of his exertions in behalf of the great body of the people than such an address as had been presented to him, if it was the pleasure of the electors again to return him to Parliament. At every election hitherto he had had the honour of being returned, without a single failure. He had felt proud of his position, and be was sure they would pardon him and not think he was disrespectful when he declared that be never bad, from his first appearance there, received a higher mark of honour or one which gave him more sincere gratification. It had always been his belief, and always his principle that, although returned to Parliament by the confidence of the electors, he went there not to represent them alone. He never disguised his feelings that he was bound to advance the interests of the country generally ; and be never considered anything more important, more grave, or more worthy consideration than the interests of the masses, who were frequently denominated the wealth of the country. They had no votes, no voice in the choice representatives, and members should therefore never neglect any means of improving their welfare, whether moral, religious, or worldly. Mr. Horsman had been his colleague for sixteen years, and he believed they had never differed, nor were they likely to differ, on any subject that was likely to interest their constituents or the non-electors of Cockermouth. He did not believe there were three votes which they were found in opposite lobbies, and if there were many they were minor points of detail. There had been no difference between them in principle or in feeling for the

---

[202] Carlisle Journal - Friday 09 April 1852

welfare of the people, and he was proud to have been so long allied with such a colleague, who had not better intentions though he might have higher abilities than he (Mr. Aglionby) had. With every wish for their welfare he begged, in conclusion, again to thank the deputation for the honour conferred upon him by the presentation of the address from the non-electors of Cockermouth. (Cheers.)

Mr. Horsman said it was necessary for him to add very little to what Mr. Aglionby had just said. He could say with great sincerity that most occasions it was very easy to make a speech, or answer an address, but be felt the present occasion too serious and too touching to allow him to do more than most sincerely and gratefully thank them for the compliment they had paid him in conjunction with his colleague. He must say, for himself, that there were various rewards which might gratify the ambition or repay the labours of public men who, whether by industry, labour, by study, or any other means, sought to advance themselves to a station of eminence or usefulness among their fellows. There might be rewards of higher character given by Ministers, Sovereigns, or Authorities, or there might be powerful classes among constituencies whose favour representatives might gain for objects of their own. But no one could say, after they bad been ' from sixteen to twenty years labouring the public service as the representatives of Cockermouth, that the approval of the working classes — of the unenfranchised — had been won otherwise than by good intentions, or indicated in those who avowed it aught else than good feeling. For himself, he would ' rather have this reward for the labours he had undertaken than the highest honour that could be bestowed upon him in ' any other quarter. It was an indication of improvement the political system of the present age, that a few years ago a ' candidate never thought of asking the opinion of the unenfranchised classes of the country. Although they were the wealth of the country — its blood, bone, and sinew — still they were one time held of little account as if they bad had ' no existence. Now they were, many them, educated and intelligent artizans, and there was no one who looked at the progress which everything we most love is making in this ' country who did not know that the best evidence of the merits of public men, and whether they did their duty, was to be found in the unbought verdict of the non-electors, who though unenfranchised, had their eyes on them — who did not lose sight of a single vote, or let pass a single speech, who, by a sort of instinct knowing what is right and what is wrong, could, at the end of sixteen years, say whether public man was honest and deserving. (Cheers.) There were various things which people cherished in families : there were family possessions, properties, and relics of various kinds; but he must say for himself that the first thing he should do would be to get the address now presented to him printed in letters of gold. (Cheers.) He would put it up in his room as the proudest possession be could enjoy; and if he bad nothing else to think of or look back to when he retired from public life, he would say, " Here, at least, I have the approval of the unenfranchised portion of the constituency of Cockermouth. It must have come from their hearts, and must find its way to mine ; and to those who come after me I will hand it down as the proudest heir-loom I am possessed of." (Cheers.)

Mr. Aglionby—l told you were always agreed; I hope I may be allowed to do the same, and that we shall not fight about the original document. (Laughter.)

The deputation then retired, and the hon. members proceeded to address the populace from the windows of the room. Mr. Aglionby, on stepping forward, was loudly cheered. ' He began by alluding to the results of the day's canvass which he said, had fully equalled, if it had not exceeded, his expectations, and by expressing pride and pleasure he had just experienced in receiving the address of the non-electors. He did wish and hope that they would give their active assistance in this difficult struggle, but, anxious as he was to receive their support, he should deeply lament if it were given by any other than constitutional means. He hoped there would nothing but argument, for be deprecated anything tending in the slightest degree to intimidation or violence. He then took exception to some hasty expressions that had been used in an anonymous placard, and said that nothing be further from the intentions of himself or his colleague than to countenance any attempt, such as was hinted at in the handbill, to prevent any 'man voting according to the dictates his conscience. Passing to another placard, the hon. Gentleman quoted the charges which it brought against him—of inconsistency in respect to the corn laws, and of opposition to Mr Henley's motion for a reduction of salaries. was proud to say that there was only two votes during twenty years service of which complaint bad been made, —(cheers)— and with respect to both of them he could give the most satisfactory explanation. Having briefly sketched the history of the various propositions for modifying and finally abolishing the Corn Laws, he showed that he had always voted on the side of the people, holding to be good policy to accept what he could when it was offered to him, and try to get more afterwards. He was advocate of cheap food long before the League came into operation—long before that great and extraordinary man Richard Cobden came forward to carry a measure which nobody but himself could carried; and he had never lost opportunity of voting in favour of diminishing the cost of the food of the people (" Cobden for ever," and cheers.) Well, " Cobden for ever,' said he, and might his principles continue to thrive and applause throughout the country; and he hoped to live to see the time when the farmers would bless the day when Cobden proposed an alteration of the Corn Laws. (Cheers.) With regard to the charge brought against him (Mr. Aglionby) of having voted against Mr. Henley's motion for a reduction of salaries, the writer of the hand-bill was right in letter, but wrong in spirit. True, he voted with the government against the motion, and he would tell them the reason why. Mr Henley was a strong Protectionist, and sat in Opposition with the party he (Mr Aglionby) had generally supported. He sat with the Tories—with the strongest supporters of pensions, sinecures, and high salaries. Mr. Henley was now at Board of Trade in Lord Derby's Administration —from which they might form a general notion of his politics. The question was that they should proceed with the business of the house. Mr. Henley moved as an amendment an address to the Queen, praying for a revision of salaries and wages paid in the public service with view to their reduction. Now no one doubted that that was a very right thing, if it had been rightly timed; but happened to be one of those things which were called clap trap motions—never intended for any good but merely to act as a vote of censure on the Government For that reason it was opposed by the Chancellor of the Exchequer; and he (Mr. Aglionby) also opposed it, and for the same reason. It was not, however, strictly, vote against the amendment: what he voted for was " the previous question,' thus indicating his opinion that the amendment was ill-timed though substantially it might be proper enough, and that it was of more importance to proceed with the other business of the house. Mr. Roebuck, Mr. Alcock, Mr. Hume, and Wakley voted for the amendment; he (Mr. Aglionby) vote with Mr. Cobden, Mr. Bright, and 167 others,. who were supposed to represent the masses of the people, for " the previous question." The hon. gentleman then proceeded to speak in favour of Law and Chancery Reform, an extension of the Suffrage, the Ballot, and reduction of taxation, and he urged his constituents to send up petitions in favour of these measures. He concluded by expressing his hope that he would be reelected in conjunction with Mr. Horsman, and that they would thus be enabled to give their support in Parliament to further measures beneficial to the great mass of the people. He was loudly cheered during the delivery of his speech. Mr. Horsman, who was also greeted with a round of cheers, next addressed the meeting. This be said was their third gathering, and it was the pleasantest of them all, for they could now compare votes and see bow matters were going on, order that the constituency of Cockermouth might be able to answer for themselves this question—what was the prospect before them, and whether or not the result of this contest was likely to establish and confirm their independence, or whether they were in future to become poor nomination borougb, as they were before they were enfranchised by the Reform Bill. He was happy to tell them that every hour's canvass enabled him to give a more agreeable answer to that question. There was great advantage in the publicity which he told them he and his colleague would court. It had brought out one fact least from their opponents—and Mr. Aglionby had truly said it was a great testimony to the integrity of public men—that after nineteen years' service all that the utmost ingenuity and hostility could pick out of the whole of his public conduct was carping objection to two unimportant votes. (Cheers.) In the course of their canvass they had not met with objections even to that extent. They did not always canvass with the same success regarded the approaching poll, because there was a considerable portion of the constituency who they knew, as a matter of course, must against them. Some even there were who, differing from them in principle, and would vote against them conscientiously, but they had not met with a single elector who had expressed any personal hostility or objection towards them: they had all given their good wishes, though they were compelled to withhold their votes. And, certainly, if anything were wanting to confirm what all this proved, the demonstration they had had that evening supplied the deficiency. (Cheers.) Having again given expression to his feelings on this point, Mr. Horsman proceeded to answer one of the anonymous handbills that had been put in circulation. There was one sentiment contained in it which he was particularly anxious to notice, because in all contests, although they ought to be carried on with earnestness and zeal, they ought to be at the same time to be carried on with fairness and good humour; and he trusted that in the course of the contest in which he had been engaged, nothing had fallen from him which could give his constituents the idea that he would adopt any other course. Now was charged in the placard with having, on Saturday evening, descended to the lowest personal and scurrilous abuse of the gallant General who was the opponent of himself and Mr. Aglionby. He was charged with having said, " What sort of an animal is our opponent?—has he a snout on his tail or tail on his " nameless part ? (Laughter.) He appealed to any one who heard him if such an expression or question fell from his lips (Cheers, and cries of "No, no.") Every body knew he did not. (Hear, hear.) What he said was this, and order that there might be no mistake about it he repeated it: he said that certain parties getting up the requisition were using his name, as he was convinced, without the General's sanction, told the town electors he was Free Trader and the country electors that he was a Protectionist. He said they were imputing to Gen. Wyndham that which as a man of honour he (Mr. Horsman) repudiated on his part. He said the gallant General could not be party to such a thing—insulting to him, and cry officious on the part of his canvassers, in taking such a liberty with their betters. (Cheers.) He also said that, General Wyndham had stated on the last occasion that he would not stand for the representation of the borough, he (Mr. Horsman) had a right to assume that he would not stand this occasion, and that there was some man of less importance in the background. He wanted to know what that man was like. They knew what the General was like— (laughter) -but here, he said, was an animal— a stranger, mysterious man, who had two faces, of two colours—so extraordinary a phenomenon that it would very interesting to know his whole anatomy. (Cheers.) He appealed to them - were not his words? ("Yes," and cheers.) After correcting other misrepresentations, Mr. Horsman said was his wish that the contest should be conducted with perfect fairness and good humour. He would not meddle with the private character of his opponents, but he would show no mercy to their politics, nor would he refrain from commenting on their public acts, public speeches, or public addresses. (Cheers.) The principle for which they were now contending was far too serious, and the interests at stake far too solemn, to allow them to stand upon any ceremony in stating what their opinions on them were; and when he found General Wyndham's agents guilty of proceeding so monstrous that which he had denounced— canvassing the town on Free Trade principles and the country on the principles of Protection—he should not refrain from denouncing it in the strongest language he could make use of. Mr. Horsman concluded his brief but telling speech amid loud cheers. The meeting was then addressed by Mr. Benson and Mr. John Richardson, jun., who in few spirited remarks pointed out the duties of the electors, and urged them to rally round their old and faithful representatives. The meeting then dispersed, but for several hours afterwards the streets were alive with groups of men canvassing the prospects of the candidates. [203]

By comparison, these elections were less spirited than previous contests. On 1 June 1840, the speeches at the hustings immediately following the poll in Cockermouth descended into chaos when Horsman and Wyndham supporters clashed. Horsman, the winner by a majority of 26 tried to speak following his victory over the General, but was drowned out by shouting

[203] Carlisle Journal - Friday 09 April 1852

and bugling from the General's supporters who demanded the General spoke first. When that did not achieve the desired outcome, he was then showered with stones and sods of earth. Wide spread pandemonium quickly descended on what was meant to be a celebratory occasion and stones began to be thrown in heavy succession in every direction.[204]

> General Wyndham and his party got to a carriage which was waiting for them outside, and galloped off, amidst a shower of stones. Several persons were lying on the ground bleeding, from wounds they had received—and the shouts of the men, and the screams of the women were terrific. Some got over hedges, others over walls—all endeavoured to fly the scene of brutal outrage. Amongst the persons who had received the greatest injury were Mr. Rudd, solicitor, and Mr. Harris, as before named. Mr. Rudd's head was severely cut, and he received a blow on the side that nearly stunned him. Mr Harris was severely cut on the cheek, and when we saw him his face was covered with blood. General Wyndham received a cut on the cheek. Mr. Horsman was twice hit with stones but not injured.[205]

The polling day took place in early July 1852 with the following results:[206]

General Henry Wyndham	160
Henry Aglionby - -	154
Edward Horsman -	147

The result of the poll was evidently a shock as Horsman was now out and Wyndham was in for the first time, as was reported on 9 July 1852.

> The Liberal cause, so triumphant in Carlisle, has sustained a partial defeat in Cockermouth. Mr. Horsman we grieve to say, is no longer member for that borough. General Wyndham has been returned, in conjunction with Mr. Aglionby, as its representative in Parliament. With the precise circumstances that have led to this untoward result we are yet imperfectly acquainted. They will probably be brought to light by a Commission under the new Bill for suppressing corrupt practices at elections. In the meantime we can do no more than record the result of the election. Our regret at the defeat of Mr. Horsman—one of the most independent and useful

---

[204] Carlisle Journal Saturday 06 June 1840

[205] Carlisle Journal Saturday 06 June 1840

[206] Adams, Henry. *Adams's Parliamentary Handbook: A Key to the Houses of Lords and Commons* 1854, http://books.google.com.au/books?id=f-YNAAAAQAAJ&dq=General%20Henry%20Wyndham%20castle&pg=PA144#v=onepage&q=General%20Henry%20Wyndham%20castle&f=false, last accessed 16/08/13

members in the House of Commons—will be shared by many, and the temporary suspension of independence in the borough he has long so faithfully served, will cause no small consternation among those who, at important crises like the present, were wont to inquire, "What will they say at Cockermouth?"[207]

Life in 1850s Cockermouth outside of election times was not as tense and turbulent. For travelling lecturers and public meetings, there were three large assembly rooms, the Globe Hotel, the Freemasons' Hall, and Hartness's Royal Assembly Room, all located in Main Street. [208]

Figure 43 Globe Hotel 1835 (Cumbria Images)

After a great deluge of rain on 11 & 12 December 1852 over the Lake District, a great flooding took place in Cockermouth in December 1852. Main Street was flooded to depth of 2 to 3 feet and a salmon was seen swimming opposite the Globe Hotel. At the "Goat" several houses were submerged up to their mantelpieces and the inhabitants had to flee quickly to avoid being swept away.[209]

> The district of which Cockermouth forms the centre, as the scene of down-pour and deluge unprecedented in the memory the present generation. The Cocker, flowing from Crummock, and the Derwent, flowing from Keswick and Bassenthwaite Lakes,

[207] Carlisle Journal - Friday 09 July 1852

[208] *Askew, John. 1866 A guide to the interesting places in and around Cockermouth*

[209] *The Edinburgh New Philosophical Journal*, Volume 55, A. and C. Black, 1853

being the two channels for carrying off the immense mass of waters collected in those mountainous districts and receiving throughout their entire course the accumulation of thousands of tributary streams, soon exceeded all bounds.... Approaching Cockermouth, the Cocker tore on down his steep incline, foaming and roaring....on reaching the bridge, adjoining the court house, the exasperated river made a sudden diversion and swept in proud style up the main street of the Market Place, which assumed the appearance itself of a river.

Isel Church it environed and forbade any service there. The Congregational Chapel in Cockermouth it shut up. The attendance at the Court House greatly thinned, the people being literally imprisoned in their houses. Such a Sabbath has not been spent in Cockermouth since the old men there were in their nurses' arms, or their grandma's went down to the Cocker in summer time to wash their snowy feet in its crystal stream. In consequence of recent rains the river Cocker rose to an unprecedented height, sweeping before it the wooden and chain bridge at the Paper Mill, the property of Mr. Harrison, farmer, likewise the bridge at Rubby Banks, on the estate of Jeremiah Spencer, Esq. washing away and destroying a considerable part of the embankment and road leading to the town, ... Considerable loss was sustained at Croft Mill woollen works, and at Wilson's hat manufactory likewise; the grocers generally were unfortunate, not having time to remove their sugar and other goods in their warehouses. Hundreds of poor families were flooded out or driven to their upper storeys, where they were compelled to stay all Sunday and Monday without fire or lights. In one house, at the Goat, there were thirteen human beings from Saturday evening till Tuesday morning prisoner in two small bed rooms. Mr. Davison, independent minister, could not get into town to preach in his chapel; his residence being at Papcastle of which, with the Lord of Derwent Bank, were all blocked out of the town, owing to the force of torrent in the Goat.

To Dr. Henry Bell every praise is due for his daring and spirited conduct in riding and often swimming on horseback from house to house rendering assistance to the inmates, and cheering them up. The Superintendent of the County Police, Mr. Brown, with his attendants rendered every assistance in their power on the occasion. At one time one fears were entertained for the Derwent bridge. The railway closed, owing to the damage sustained, and the Directors are running a coach three times a day to meet the Workington line. ... It was amusing to see the anxiety of the good town's folks looking out for the bakers bringing them their Sunday dinner, wading from house to house up to the middle in water. Fortunately, there has been no loss of life—but much property is destroyed. [210]

In 1856, the owners of the mills in Cockermouth gave their workers a holiday on the Saturday and paid for a train trip to Carlisle, but not the return trip!

---

[210] Carlisle Patriot - Saturday 18 December 1852

Pleasure Trips.—On Saturday last Messrs. Harris and Son, thread manufacturers, Cockermouth, gave the hands in their employ, (numbering upwards of 600 men, women, and children),a holiday, and paid their fares by an excursion train to this city. The Rail way Company also granted return tickets at reduced fares, of which a considerable number availed themselves, including the operatives of Mr. Joseph Grave, from the Fitz Mills, and those of Mr. Pearson, of the Croft Mills. The train, with upwards of 1,000 passengers, left the railway station, Cockermouth, at half-past six a.m., and returned a little before nine p.m. The day was remarkably fine, and the excursionists appeared highly delighted with their trip.[211]

What became of Henry will be the subject of the next section. His brother, Joseph the younger, had travelled to Great and Little Clifton about six miles east of Cockermouth to marry Sarah Fleming on 5 May 1850, but settled down in Cockermouth in Brewery Lane, next door to his parents. Joseph in the 1850s was a flax thread maker by trade, but later employed as a shale layer for the railway. The thread made from the flax plant, was used to create cloth. Joseph and Sarah's children were all born in Cockermouth, William (1851), Agnes (1853), John (1855), Robert Henry (1860) and Sarah Hannah (1862). By 1861 were residing in Wyndham Row.

In the 1874 Electoral Register for the Borough of Cockermouth, Joseph the elder is mentioned as qualifying to be eligible to vote as he owned his house in Brewery Lane, which explains why his family stayed at this address for over 25 years. It is also possible, but less likely, that he may have rented the house, as the 1832 Reform Act gave the franchise to householders who paid more than £10 in rent per annum. The 1867 Reform Act enfranchised in the boroughs all householders who paid poor rates and tenants who paid £10 or more in rent. This later Act may explain Joseph's eligibility to vote. It is interesting to note that in the same electoral register that a Solomon Cragg (which Solomon is a mystery) living in Main Street was eligible to vote as well.

In the 1928 letter (written by his grandson John) Joseph was described as a Sunday School teacher and Church of England Sunday School Superintendent. An article in the *Carlisle Journal* on 26 February gives a small insight to his character.

Treat to Sunday School Teachers and the Cockermouth Church Choir.—On Tuesday evening last, the Rev. H.L.Puxley, curate of All Saints Church', entertained upwards of 80 teachers and singers to tea in the General Sunday School. The rev. gentleman was very ably assisted by a few of the senior lady teachers, to whose valuable services in decorating the room, preparing and serving out the tea and other good things, the company were much indebted. In addition the company were agreeably entertained

---

[211] Friday 25 July 1856 , *Carlisle Journal* , Cumbria, England

by the rev. gentleman showing his magic lantern, which showed a number of pleasing missionary views in West Africa, North-west America, India, China, and New Zealand, Schools, scenery, &c, &c. The Church Choir very ably sang a few anthems, &c. The meeting was addressed by several of the teachers. Mr. Joseph Cragg, in a humourous speech introduced the anecdote of the Rev. R. and Mrs. Hill. The Rev. Mr. Erie, complimented the meeting upon the good humour and friendly feeling which prevailed amongst them. A unanimous vote of thanks was tendered to the Rev. H. L. Puxley, for his kindness; and the choir concluded the happy meeting by singing the National Anthem.[212]

Both Joseph the elder and his wife, Hannah, died only 15 days apart in 1878. Joseph passed away on 2 July and Hannah on 17 July at their Brewery Lane residence. At the time of his death, Joseph was as a "coal carter" by trade.[213] This usually meant he had a horse and cart by which he transported coal. This may have been from the nearby coalfields three miles away to different locations or from a local depo to places in town that used the coal. The cause of his death was two months of 'acute bronchitis'. While it is known he was born in 1803 his age at death was recorded as 77 years, when he was actually 74 years of age. George Booth, Hannah the younger's husband, was present at Joseph the elder's death. He was present again 15 days later, when Hannah the elder passed away from fourteen days of 'phthisis pulmonalis', which was a form of wasting disease that affected the lungs such as tuberculosis. According to the same letter, both Joseph and his wife are buried in the Churchyard.

[212] Carlisle Journal - Tuesday 26 February 1861
[213] Joseph Cragg's Death Certificate

Chapter Nine - Henry Cragg (1827-1903) and Mary Anne Geddes (1829-1868)

Joseph and Hannah's second child and second son, Henry, was born 5 March 1827 and christened 8 April that same year in the Independent Chapel at Cockermouth.

In 1841, at the age of 14, Henry was employed in a local woollen mill. His brother Isaac was a weaver's apprentice at 16, so it is quite possible he had to wait a few years before he too had an apprenticeship. Only three months was required to learn the weaving business, but no doubt, the apprenticeships lasted much longer.

On 1 March 1846 Henry, just four days shy of 19, married 17 year old Mary Anne Geddes (or Gaddes) at Gretna Green in Scotland. The service was provided by Simon Lang.

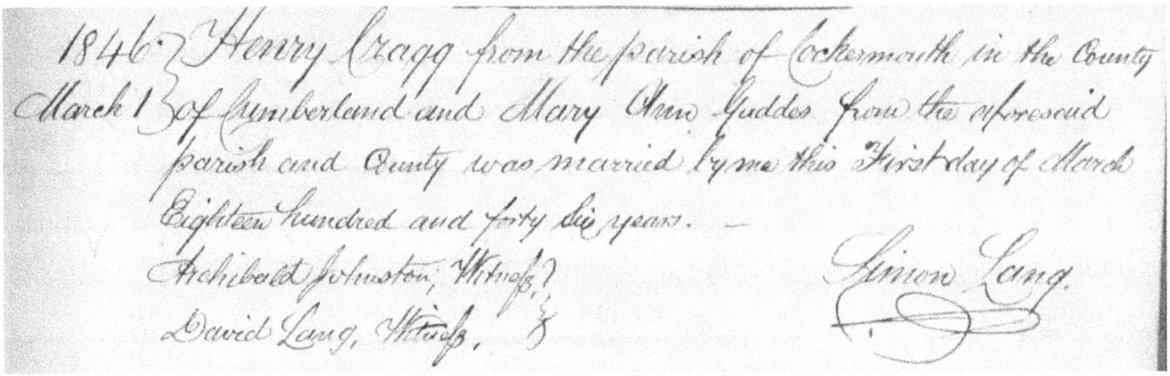
1846 March 1 } Henry Cragg from the parish of Cockermouth in the County of Cumberland and Mary Ann Geddes from the aforesaid parish and County was married by me this First day of March Eighteen hundred and forty six years. —

Archibald Johnston, Witness }
David Lang, Witness, }

Simon Lang.

Figure 44 Gretna Green, Scotland, Marriage Registers, 1794-1895

Situated just over the border with Scotland in "debatable land", Gretna Green was often the destination of couples who wished to marry without parental consent. After 1753, when English law forbade irregular marriages, a number of people who objected to marrying in a church or were below the legal age of 21 wed in border centres, of which Gretna was the most famous, where the couple's own consent to marriage before witnesses was legal under Scottish Law. Scottish Law held that the legal age without parental consent was 16 years. Marriages were conducted by self-appointed ministers at the border toll booths along the few roads into Scotland. The "priests", as they called themselves, often had other jobs giving rise to the stories of being married over an anvil by the village Blacksmith. Simon Lang was one of the best known "anvil priests" or "blacksmith priests" at the time. He was born in Springfield (a village adjacent to Gretna Green) to David Lang who had commenced the Gretna Green marriage trade in 1792. After his father's death in 1827, Simon Lang became the only 'Blacksmith Priest' of importance who was actually born in the village. Lang was described as "a kind of happy medium, neither tall nor short, in face somewhat spare and not much otherwise in limb". He had a keen sense of humour and had a reputation for integrity. Like other priests of the time, he saw a substantial drop in the marriage trade around 1837, and turned to weaving and smuggling to support his family. He managed to remain in the "priesthood" until his passing in 1872.[214]

Mary Anne Geddes had been born in Tyrone, Ireland. Her Father Alexander Geddes had also been born in the same county in Cooktown. However, their family line originated from Aberdeenshire, Scotland. Between 1847-1851, during the great Potato Famine, there was the emigration of one million people from Ireland. A further one million died of starvation. In the midst of all this, Joseph and Mary met, married, and gave birth to their first son Joseph Henry Cragg on 23 January 1847.

Henry and Mary Anne went on to have a further five children in Cockermouth, with the last born in 1858. In order, their children were Joseph Henry, William, Martha, John, Alexander and Hannah (or Anna). Unfortunately, John died as an infant and buried at All Saints by Rev. Edward Fawcett on 7 January 1855.

In the 1851 census, they are shown to be living in Castle Street, just around the corner from Joseph and Hannah, who were Henry's parents. Instead of merely listed as 'employed in a woollen mill' as he was in 1841, Henry was now a 'hand loom weaver/woollery' just as his father was in the same census. In 1858, there were two woollen factories in Cockermouth. One was owned by Joseph Graves, and operated in Waterloo Street (Sand Went) and at Fitz Mills. The Waterloo Street mill was called was Graves's Mill and was built in the 1820s. At one stage, it had a water wheel powered by a race from the River Derwent. It was later demolished in 1981.[215]

---

[214] http://www.gretnagreen.com/david-and-simon-lang-a757, last accessed Oct 6th 2013.

[215] J. Bernard Bradbury, Cockermouth and District in Old Photographs, 1994, Alan Sutton Publishing Ltd., Gloucestershire, England.

Figure 45 Graves Mill: Derwent River and Waterloo St frontages (J. Bernard Bradbury)

The other mill, Croft Mill, was situated on the western bank of the Cocker River and owned by John Pearson.[216] At the east end of South Street, a narrow court, closed in by a massive wooden gate, was the chief approach to Mr. John Pearson's Woollen Mill. In 1858, Henry worked at Croft Mill, which was eventually converted into flats in the 1970's. In 1859, Henry was recorded as an 'engine driver', and since he worked at Croft Mill, he would have spent much of his time in the engine house (see Figure 47) at the northern end of the Mill.

Figure 46 Croft Mill on the west bank of the Cocker. (J. Bernard Bradbury)

---

[216] 1858 Post Office Directory Vol. 1

Between 1851 and 1859, Henry had made a career change from handloom weaver to engine driver, which is interesting as it hints at the inroads steam driven power looms were making into the woollen industry. The wool weaving industry was very slow to pick up the power loom, as the weaker woollen fibres broke easily on these crude machines. Woollen hand weaving was therefore still preferable long after cotton had gone over to the power-looms. By 1866, the chief manufactures of the town were relatively unchanged - woollen fabrics, hats, and linen thread. [217]

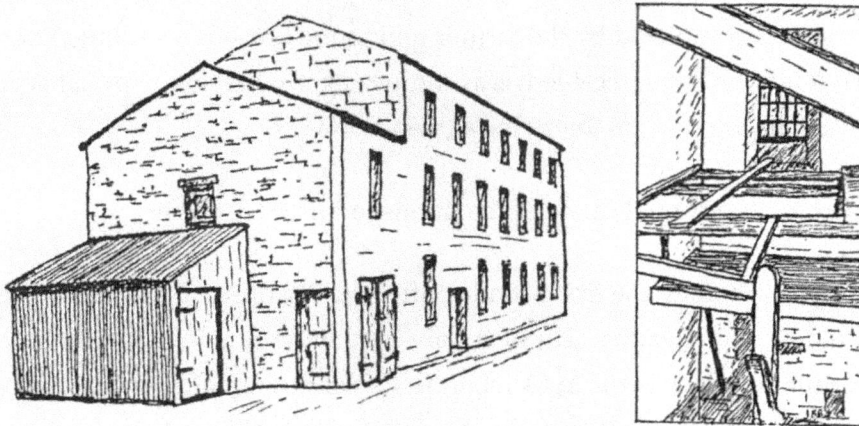

Figure 47 Croft Mill's Engine House and Engine Room (J. Bernard Bradbury)

In March 1851, Henry's and Mary Anne's young sons, Joseph Henry and William were living with their parents as expected. Mary Anne's mother, Martha Cooper, who had remarried to William Cooper, was residing with them as well and employed as a bobbin winder. Mary Anne's 20-year-old brother, Thomas Geddes, who was agricultural labourer, was visiting the night of the census. Agricultural labourers were paid by the day or week and were often provided meals; however, they tended not to live on the farms they worked. Where Thomas worked and where he was visiting from is not known, though it is certain he was born in Ireland. By 1850, the wages of agricultural labourers in Cumberland were about the average for the country as a whole, but more than 50 percent above the average for the southern counties.[218] Thomas may have been hired at the regular hiring and pleasure fairs for farm-servants, male and female held on Whit Monday and Martinmas Monday.[219] Labourers were generally hired for a year or six months at a time. In between periods of service, hired labourers enjoyed a week's holiday, which they usually spent visiting relatives. However, the

---

[217] *Askew, John. 1866 A guide to the interesting places in and around Cockermouth*

[218] James Caird, English Agriculture in 1850-51, 1852, London as cited in C.M.L Bouch and G.P. Jones, The Lake Counties, 1500-1800 by, 1961, Manchester University Press.

[219] *Askew, John. 1866 A guide to the interesting places in and around Cockermouth*

1851 census was taken on Sunday March 30, which did not coincide with a regular week's holiday for farm labourers. The hiring fairs themselves were quaint rituals where:

> "... the men and women stand in the market place on the appointed day, the former wearing some token in their coats or hats, a straw generally...as an indication that they were unhired. The farmers pass among them, and selecting likely-looking man or woman, the bargaining for wages commence [sic] and on an agreement being come to the bargain is completed by the farmer giving the servant a shilling, known as 'Yearl' or 'Arl', which on being received, is a binding acknowledgment for half a year's service, to the next hiring day, on the terms agreed upon."[220]

Other key events on the annual calendar (as published in 1866) were:

> February 18—horses; the first Monday after the 5th of April—a show of entire horses; first Wednesday after the 12th of April—cattle; the first Wednesday in May—cattle, and fortnightly afterwards to October; first Wednesday after the 17th of August, and first Wednesday after the 20th of September—sheep and lambs. October 10 (Michaelmas day)—a large horse and cattle fair. Few towns of the same size as Cockermouth are so fortunately situated in this respect; and the opportunity that buyers and sellers have of meeting together in a convenient place must result in no small benefit to the trade of Cockermouth.

The year, 1859, was to be a one that marked separation from family, friends, Cockermouth and finally England as Henry took his family on a journey to Sydney, Australia. On Tuesday 15 March 1859, John Askew of Brigham, the author of "Australia and New Zealand" presented a lecture at Cockermouth's Mechanics' Institute on "Life Australia: past and present, savage and civilised". No doubt, Henry Cragg was in attendance and listening attentively to what was judged to be a "very interesting lecture".[221] Between 1851 and 1861, Cockermouth's population would fall dramatically from 5,775 to 5,388 (-6.7%) after the town had a 16.9% increase in population between 1841 and 1851.[222]

In 1927, a nephew of Henry's named John Cragg, wrote a letter to his son John. In it, he recalled that when his Uncle Henry left for Australia in 1859, a cat had been left behind in Cockermouth and placed in the care of a grandmother. Another letter referred to the fact that

---

[220] F.W. Garnett, Westmorland Agriculture 1800-1900, 1912, Kendal as cited in C.M.L Bouch and G.P. Jones, The Lake Counties, 1500-1800 by, 1961, Manchester University Press.

[221] Cumberland Pacquet, and Ware's Whitehaven Advertiser - Tuesday 22 March 1859

[222] Marshall, J. D. (John Duncan) & Walton, John K 1981, *The Lake Counties from 1830 to the mid-twentieth century : a study in regional change*, Manchester University Press, Manchester [Great Manchester]

the family were taken to the train station by donkey cart. The Cockermouth & Workington Railway was a railway between the towns of Workington and Cockermouth established by an Act of Parliament in 1845. Built primarily to carry coals from the pits of West Cumberland to the port at Workington for shipment by sea, it consisted of a single-tracked line of eight and a half miles in length and was opened for service in 1847. The western terminus was the Whitehaven Junction Railway station in Workington, while the eastern terminus lay at Cockermouth (C&W) railway station. This station opened on 28 April 1847 and closed on 2 January 1865.

Thomas, Mary Ann's brother, had already immigrated to Australia in 1854, on the *Araminta* with his wife Mary and baby Mary Jane. Their brother, John Gaddis, born 1823, had ventured a decade earlier to Australia, in 1842. By 1859, both of Mary Ann's brothers resided in Sydney.

Chapter Ten - Those Who Stayed

W hat was to become of the Cragg families that stayed in England, while Henry and his family went to seek their fortune Australia? The dramatic dispersion of the Cragg family is evident in the 1881 UK census. Only a handful were still living in Cumberland (Cumbria) by this time. According to the Oxford Guide to Family History, Cumberland's inhabitants shared the unprecedented population growth in England during the 19th Century. The county experienced an influx of immigrants, which in turn placed more pressure on the limited resources and employment opportunities.

> 'Over 5,000 agricultural labourers and female servants left the Cumbrian countryside during the three decades following 1851, and this outflow was sustained during the remainder of the Victorian and Edwardian period. The younger sons of farmers and rural craftsmen joined the labourers and servants in this mass departure. By 1891 well over 100,000 Cumbrian-born people were living in other parts of England and Wales; they corresponded to almost a third of the total population of Cumbria at that time...'[223]

Most often, the Cumbrian migrants resettled in the nearest county, settling in an industrial town. The most popular destination was Liverpool in Lancashire (now in Mersyside County) which hosted 5,801 Cumbrians. Within the 1881 census for Lancashire, fragments of the Cragg family may be found in that county.

Those who remained in Cumberland where only a few. Though the numbers may be deceptive, as the Cragg name was naturally lost when female members married.

In the 1881 census for Cumberland, Solomon Cragg, the son of John Cragg, was lodging at 24 Prospect Row, Cleator. The census stated that he was 44 years of age and employed as a factory operator. Residing with him was his 12-year-old daughter, Sarah, a scholar who had also been born in Cockermouth.

In Cockermouth on Waterloo Street, three houses from Askew Court, Sarah Cragg (wife of Isaac Cragg) aged 54 was living with her son Joseph William Cragg, aged 21. Sarah's occupation was 'hat trimmer', while Joseph William was a carter. Sarah was deemed the head of the household, and a widow, which meant some tragedy had befallen Isaac.

---

[223] David Hey, The Oxford Guide to Family History, 1993, Oxford University Press.

The 1891 Census gives a clear indication of where the highest concentration of Cragg families were at that time in England. In the census, 2,062 Cragg Households existed in England and Wales.

County	Cragg Households	%	County	Cragg Households	%
Lancashire	599	29	Hampshire	29	1
Cheshire	148	7	Cumberland	26	1
Nottinghamshire	178	9	Staffordshire	25	1
Lincolnshire	179	9	Surrey	20	1
London	128	6	Derbyshire	19	1
Westmorland	106	5	Devon	18	1
Sussex	79	4	Worcestershire	16	1
Leicestershire	62	3	Northumberland	15	1
Durham	45	3	Middlesex	14	1
Warwickshire	46	2	Kent	11	1
Cambridgeshire	30	1	Other	269	13

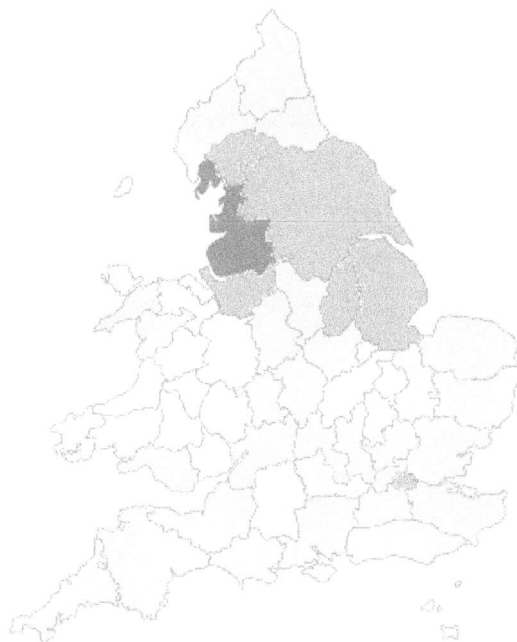

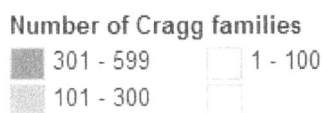

Number of Cragg families
301 - 599   1 - 100
101 - 300

from the 1891 England and Wales Census Data

One hundred years on from 1891, the UK telephone books gave a clear idea of the top 10 Cragg counties in 1991:

County	Cragg Households	Population
Lancashire	147	1,365,100
Cheshire	71	937,300
Nottinghamshire	63	980,600
Lincolnshire	38	573,900
Mersyside	38	1,376,800
Leicestershire	34	860,500
West Midlands	29	2,500,400
London, Greater	28	6,378,600
West Yorkshire	25	1,984,700
Cumbria	22	486,900

The largest concentration of Cragg families in 1991 was in Lancashire, which agrees with the migration patterns of Cumbrian people in the late to middle 1800s. It is quite probable that the majority of the Cragg family left behind in England reside in this county.

Appendix A – 1841 Census Data (6 June 1841).

1841 Cockermouth, Sand Went (corner of Waterloo Street).

Names of each person who abode therein the preceding night.	Age and Sex		Profession Trade, Employment, or of Independent Means.	Where Born.	
	Male	Female		Whether Born in The same County	Whether Born in Scotland, Ireland or Foreign Parts
Isaac Cragg	70		Tanner	Y	
Ruth do		75		Y	
Sarah do	40		Thread Reeler	Y	
Isaac Carr	20		Waller	Y	
Jacob Bonson	10			Y	

1841 Cockermouth, Main Street. Joseph Cragg (son of Isaac and Ruth)

Names of each person who abode therein the preceding night.	Age and Sex		Profession Trade, Employment, or of Independent Means.	Where Born.	
	Male	Female		Whether Born in The same County	Whether Born in Scotland, Ireland or Foreign Parts
Joseph Cragg	35		Weaver	Y	
Hannah do		35		Y	
Issac do	16		Weaver App.	Y	
Henry do	14		Employed in a woollen Mill	Y	
John do	10			Y	
Joseph do	12			Y	
Robert do	7			Y	
William do	4			Y	

1841 Cockermouth, Waterloo Street. John Cragg (son of Isaac and Ruth)

Names of each person who abode therein the preceding night.	Age and Sex		Profession Trade, Employment, or of Independent Means.	Where Born.	
	Male	Female		Whether Born in The same County	Whether Born in Scotland, Ireland or Foreign Parts
John Cragg	49		Waller	Y	
Jane do		48		Y	
Betsey do		22	Thread Reeler	Y	
Isaac do	20		Waller	Y	
Jane do		13		Y	
Sarah do		9		Y	
Solomon do	5			Y	
Thomas do	2			Y	

1841 Cockermouth, Gallow Barrow. Ruth Cragg (daughter of Isaac and Ruth)

Names of each person who abode therein the preceding night.	Age and Sex		Profession Trade, Employment, or of Independent Means.	Where Born.	
	Male	Female		Whether Born in The same County	Whether Born in Scotland, Ireland or Foreign Parts
John Birkett	40		Shoe Maker	Y	
Ruth do		40		Y	
Isaac do	16		Joiner Ap.	Y	
William do	14		Nailor Ap.	Y	
Johnston do	12		Woollen Mill	Y	
John do	10			Y	
David do	4			Y	
Ruth do		6m		Y	

1841 Maryport, Canonby. Solomon Cragg (son of Isaac and Ruth)

Names of each person who abode therein the preceding night.	Age and Sex		Profession Trade, Employment, or of Independent Means.	Where Born.	
	Male	Female		Whether Born in The same County	Whether Born in Scotland, Ireland or Foreign Parts
Solomon Cragg	30		Publican	Y	
Elizabeth do		30		Y	
Thomas Carminson	60		Tailor	Y	
John Waterford	70		Ag Lab.	Y	

1841 Great Broughton, Standing Stone, Elizabeth Cragg (daughter of Isaac and Ruth)

Names of each person who abode therein the preceding night.	Age and Sex		Profession Trade, Employment, or of Independent Means.	Where Born.	
	Male	Female		Whether Born in The same County	Whether Born in Scotland, Ireland or Foreign Parts
William Hodgson	35		Ag Lab.	Y	
Elizabeth do		30		Y	
Betsy Hodgson		5		Y	
Henry do	4			Y	
Isaac do	2			Y	

Appendix B – 1851 Census Data (30 March 1851)

1851 Cockermouth, Sullart Street. Ruth Cragg (daughter of Isaac and Ruth)

Names of each person who abode therein the preceding night.	Relation to Head of Family	Condition	Age of		Rank, Profession or Occupation	Where Born	Whether Blind, Deaf or Dumb
			Males	Females			
John Birkett	Head	Married	50		Shoe Maker Journeyman	Norman Cross, Huntingshire	
Ruth do	Wife	Married		50	Bobin Winder	Cumberland Cockermouth	
John do	Son	U	19		Weaver Cotton	do	
Thomas do	Son	U	16		Thread Maker Flax Mill	do	
Ruth do	Daughter			10	Scholar	do	
Richard do	Son		7			do	

1851 Cockermouth, Brewery Lane. Joseph Cragg (son of Isaac and Ruth)

Names of each person who abode therein the preceding night.	Relation to Head of Family	Condition	Age of		Rank, Profession or Occupation	Where Born	Whether Blind, Deaf or Dumb
			Males	Females			
Joseph Cragg snr	Head	Married	48		Hand Loom Weaver Woollen	Cockermouth	
Hannah do	Wife	Married		48		do	
John do	Son	U	18		? app.	do	
Robert do	Son	U	16		Shoemaker app.	do	
Hannah do	Daughter	U		5	Scholar	do	

1851 Cockermouth, Brewery Lane. Joseph Cragg (son of Joseph and Hannah). Next door.

Names of each person who abode therein the preceding night.	Relation to Head of Family	Condition	Age of		Rank, Profession or Occupation	Where Born	Whether Blind, Deaf or Dumb
			Males	Females			
Joseph Cragg jnr	Head	Married	22		Flax Thread Maker	Cockermouth	
Sarah do	Wife	Married		22		Whitehaven	

1851 Cockermouth, Castle Street (near Pearson's yard). Henry Cragg (son of Joseph and Hannah).

Names of each person who abode therein the preceding night.	Relation to Head of Family	Condition	Age of		Rank, Profession or Occupation	Where Born	Whether Blind, Deaf or Dumb
			Males	Females			
Henry Cragg	Head	Married	34		Hand loom weaver Woollen	Cockermouth	
Mary A. do	Wife	Married		32		Ireland	
Joseph H. do	Son		4			Cockermouth	
William do	Son		2			Cockermouth	
Martha Cooper	Wife's Mother	Married		40	Bobbin winder	Ireland	
Thomas Geddes	Visitor	U	20		Ag. Labourer	Ireland	

1851 Kendal, Stricklandgate. Isaac Cragg (son of Joseph and Hannah).

Names of each person who abode therein the preceding night.	Relation to Head of Family	Condition	Age of		Rank, Profession or Occupation	Where Born	Whether Blind, Deaf or Dumb
			Males	Females			
Isaac Cragg	Head	Married	26		Hand loom weaver Woollen	Cockermouth	
Ann do	Wife	Married		25		Ireland	
Ann do	Daughter			9m		Westmoreland	

1851 Dearham, Solomon Craigg (son of Isaac and Ruth).

Names of each person who abode therein the preceding night.	Relation to Head of Family	Condition	Age of		Rank, Profession or Occupation	Where Born	Whether Blind, Deaf or Dumb
			Males	Females			
Solomon Craigg	Head	Married	42		Railway Labourer	Cockermouth	
Elizabeth do	Wife	Married		42	Inn Keeper	Tallentire	

1851 Dearham, Boustead Buildings. Elizabeth Cragg (daughter of Isaac and Ruth)

Names of each person who abode therein the preceding night.	Relation to Head of Family	Condition	Age of		Rank, Profession or Occupation	Where Born	Whether Blind, Deaf or Dumb
			Males	Females			
William Hodgson	Head	Married	48		Banksman	Tallentire	
Elizabeth do	Wife	Married		40		Cockermouth	
Betsy do	Daughter	U		15		Standingstone	
Henry do	Son		13			Standingstone	
Isaac do	Son		12			Standingstone	
William do	Son		9			Standingstone	
John do	Son		7			Standingstone	
Sarah do	Daughter			5		Dearham	
Thomas do	Son		3			Dearham	
Jane do	Daughter			1		Dearham	

1851 Dearham, Boustead Buildings. Ruth Cragg (daughter of John and Jane Cragg)

Names of each person who abode therein the preceding night.	Relation to Head of Family	Condition	Age of		Rank, Profession or Occupation	Where Born	Whether Blind, Deaf or Dumb
			Males	Females			
Henry Hodgson	Head	Married	42		Labourer	Tallentire	
Ruth do	Wife	Married		36		Cockermouth	
John do	Son	U	14		Agricultural Laborer	Tallentire	
Betsy do	Daughter			12	Scholar	Dovenby	
Jane do	Daughter			12	Scholar	Dovenby	
Henry do	Son		8		Scholar	Dovenby	
Sarah Ann do	Daughter			4		Dovenby	
Helen do	Daughter			10m		Dovenby	

1851 Applethwaite, Knots. Isaac Cragg (son of John and Jane Cragg)

Names of each person who abode therein the preceding night.	Relation to Head of Family	Condition	Age of		Rank, Profession or Occupation	Where Born	Whether Blind, Deaf or Dumb
			Males	Females			
William Harrinson	Head	Married	52		Stone Mason employing 12 Men	Westmoreland, Windermere	
Ann do	Wife	Married		57		Westmoreland, Windermere	
Mary Ann do	Daughter	U		18	Dress Maker	Westmoreland, Windermere	
Thomas do	Son		16		Stonemason	Westmoreland, Windermere	
Joshua do	Son		12		Scholar	Westmoreland, Windermere	
Thomas Airey	App.		19		Stonemason App.	Westmoreland, Windermere	
Isaac Cragg	Lodger			27	Stone Mason Journey Man.	Cumberland Cockermouth	
Robert Holme	Lodger			28	Bobbin prepairer	Westmoreland, Heversham	

1851 Cockermouth, Sand Lane Jane Cragg (nee Oswald) (widow of John Cragg)

Names of each person who abode therein the preceding night.	Relation to Head of Family	Condition	Age of		Rank, Profession or Occupation	Where Born	Whether Blind, Deaf or Dumb
			Males	Females			
Jane Cragg	Head	Wid		59	On parish relief	Cockermouth	
Solomon do	Son	U		15	Employed Parting Thread	Cockermouth	
Thomas do	Son			13	Employed Parting Thread	Cockermouth	

Appendix C – Descendants of Isaac Cragg (1770-1858)

Generation 1

1. ISAAC[1] CRAGG was born about 1770 in Crosthwaite, Cumberland, England (Poor House in Keswick). He died on 28 Nov 1858 in Dearham,Cumberland,England (Cause of Death: "Old age"). He married Ruth Osburne, daughter of Solomon Osburne and Ruth Messenger, on 29 Dec 1793 in Saint Michael,Workington,Cumberland,England (St Michael, Workington, Cumberland). She was born about 1765 in Cumberland, England. She died on 15 Dec 1849 in Sand Lane, Cockermouth, Cumberland, England (12 hours of Diarrhoea).

    Isaac Cragg and Ruth Osburne had the following children:

     i. SARAH[2] CRAGG was born in Feb 1799 in Cockermouth, Cumberland, England. She died in Mar 1843 in Cockermouth, Cumberland, United Kingdom.

     ii. MARY CRAGG was born about 1794 in Cockermouth, Cumberland, England.

2. iii. JOHN CRAGG was born on 17 Jul 1795 in Cockermouth, Cumberland, England. He died on 18 Jan 1849 in Cockermouth, Cumberland, England. He married Jane Oswald on 12 Nov 1815. She was born in 1796 in Cockermouth, Cumberland, England. She died about Dec 1872 in Cockermouth, Cumberland, England.

     iv. JANE CRAGG was born on 15 Mar 1799 in Cockermouth, Cumberland, England.

3. v. RUTH CRAGG was born on 18 Feb 1801 in Cockermouth, Cumberland, England. She died on 17 Apr 1870 in Birkett Buildings, Cockermouth, Cumberland, England. She married (1) JOHN BIRKETT, son of William Birket and Sarah Johnston, on 05 May 1821 in Brigham Parish, Cumberland, England. He was born in 1801 in Norman Cross, Huntingdonshire, England. He died on 25 Dec 1864 in Sullart Street, Cockermouth, Cumberland, England. She married (2) HENRY HODGSON, son of Henry Hodgson and Elizabeth Elliott, on 06 Aug 1836 in Bridekirk Parish, Cumberland, England. He was born on 30 May 1806 in Bridekirk Cumberland. He died in 1879.

4. vi. JOSEPH CRAGG was born on 04 Apr 1803 in Cockermouth, Cumberland, England. He died on 02 Jul 1878 in Cockermouth, Cumberland, England (Acute Bronchitis). He married Hannah Grave, daughter of Henry Grave and Margaret, on 01 Dec 1823 in Brigham Parish, Cumberland, England. She was born on 20 Mar 1803 in Cockermouth, Cumberland, England. She died on 17 Jul 1878 in Cockermouth, Cumberland, England (Phthisis Pulmonalis).

     vii. ISAAC CRAGG was born on 02 Sep 1805 in Cockermouth, Cumberland, England. He died in Nov 1806 in Cockermouth, Cumberland, England.

5. viii. SOLOMON CRAGG was born on 17 Mar 1809 in Cockermouth, Cumberland, England. He died on 06 Feb 1863 in Dearham, Cumberland, England (Cumberland Pacquet, and Ware's Whitehaven Advertiser - Tuesday 17 February 1863 pg 5. Dearham, on 6th inst, Mr. Solomon Cragg, aged 54 years). He married Elizabeth Hodgson, daughter of Henry Hodgson and Elizabeth Elliott, on 09 Jun 1832 in Bridekirk Parish, Cumberland, England. She was born on 07 Jul 1808 in Bridekirk Cumberland.

6. ix. ELIZABETH CRAGG was born on 24 Dec 1810 in Cockermouth, Cumberland, England. She died on 10 Jun 1875 in Cumberland, England. She married (2) WILLIAM HODGSON, son of Henry Hodgson and Elizabeth Elliott, on 25 May 1833 in Bridekirk

Parish, Cumberland, England. He was born on 07 Oct 1804 in Tallentire, Cumberland, England. He died in Oct 1858 in Cockermouth, Cumberland, United Kingdom.

Generation 2

2. JOHN[2] CRAGG (Isaac[1]) was born on 17 Jul 1795 in Cockermouth, Cumberland, England. He died on 18 Jan 1849 in Cockermouth, Cumberland, England. He married Jane Oswald on 12 Nov 1815. She was born in 1796 in Cockermouth, Cumberland, England. She died about Dec 1872 in Cockermouth, Cumberland, England.

    John Cragg and Jane Oswald had the following children:

    7. i.   RUTH[3] CRAGG was born about 1817 in Cockermouth, Cumberland, England. She died in 1901 in Cumberland, England. She married Henry Hodgson on 06 Aug 1836 in Cumberland, England. He was born in 1808 in Tallantire, Cumberland, England. He died in 1879 in Cumberland, England.

    8. ii. ELIZABETH CRAGG was born on 28 Mar 1819 in Cockermouth, Cumberland, England. She died in Mar 1881 in Whitehaven, Cumberland, England. She married (1) WILLIAM HODGSON. He was born in 1804 in Cumberland, England. She married (2) WILLIAM GRAVE, son of Joseph Grave, on 19 Aug 1843 in All Saints, Cockermouth, Cumberland, Eng (At Cockermouth, on Friday the 18th inst., Mr. Wm. Grave, shoemaker, to Miss Elizabeth Cragg.). He was born about 1812 in Cockermouth, Cumberland, England.

        iii. ISAAC CRAGG was born on 22 Jul 1821 in Cockermouth, Cumberland, England.

        iv. JOHN CRAGG was born on 10 Dec 1826 in Cockermouth, Cumberland, England.

        v.   JANE CRAGG was born on 19 Jul 1829 in Cockermouth, Cumberland, England.

        vi. SARAH CRAGG was born on 08 Jul 1832 in Cockermouth, Cumberland, England. She died on 09 Mar 1843 in Cockermouth, Cumberland, England.

    9. vii. SOLOMON CRAGG was born on 03 Apr 1836 in Cockermouth, Cumberland, England. He died in Apr 1894 in Cumberland, England.

    10. viii. THOMAS CRAGG was born in Oct 1838 in Cockermouth, Cumberland, England. He married Susannah Digney, daughter of Bernard Digney and Mary, on 15 Feb 1858 in Cockermouth, Cumberland, England (vol 10b page 535). She was born in 1842 in Whitehaven, Cumberland, England.

3. RUTH[2] CRAGG (Isaac[1]) was born on 18 Feb 1801 in Cockermouth, Cumberland, England. She died on 17 Apr 1870 in Birkett Buildings, Cockermouth, Cumberland, England. She married (1) JOHN BIRKETT, son of William Birket and Sarah Johnston, on 05 May 1821 in Brigham Parish, Cumberland, England. He was born in 1801 in Norman Cross, Huntingdonshire, England. He died on 25 Dec 1864 in Sullart Street, Cockermouth, Cumberland, England. She married (2) HENRY HODGSON, son of Henry Hodgson and Elizabeth Elliott, on 06 Aug 1836 in Bridekirk Parish, Cumberland, England. He was born on 30 May 1806 in Bridekirk Cumberland. He died in 1879.

    John Birkett and Ruth Cragg had the following children:

        i.   JANE[3] BIRKETT was born in 1837 in Cockermouth, Cumberland, England. She died in Dec 1837 in Cockermouth, Cumberland, England.

        ii. WILLIAM BIRKETT was born about 1821 in Cockermouth, Cumberland, England. He died about 1823 in Cockermouth, Cumberland, England.

    11. iii. JOSEPH BIRKETT was born on 19 Jan 1823 in Cockermouth, Cumberland, England. He died on 17 Nov 1901 in Carbondale, Lackawanna, Pennsylvania, USA. He married (1) SARAH J HEWITSON on 15 Sep 1897 in Buffalo, New York, USA. She was born in

Apr 1851 in Pennsylvania,USA. He married (2) ANN DRUMMOND on 26 Dec 1842 in All Saints Church,Cockermouth, England. She was born on 13 Mar 1823 in Cockermouth, Cumberland, England. She died on 19 Sep 1895 in Carbondale City,Lackawanna,Pennsylvania.

iv. SARAH BIRKETT was born about 1830 in Cockermouth, Cumberland, England. She died on 20 May 1832 in Cockermouth, Cumberland, England.

12.   v. THOMAS BIRKETT was born about 1834 in Cockermouth, Cumberland, England. He died on 26 Dec 1894 in Carbondale City,Lackawanna,Pennsylvania. He married Helen Eliza Crocker about 1874 in Lackawanna,Carbondale,PA. She was born in Jan 1844 in Pennsylvania,USA. She died on 20 Nov 1916 in Carbondale, Lackawanna, Pennsylvania, USA.

13.   vi. RICHARD BIRKETT was born on 03 Jun 1843 in Cockermouth, Cumberland, England. He died in Jun 1915 in Cockermouth, Cumberland, England. He married Margaret Quin, daughter of William Quin and Ellen Queen, in 1865 in Cockermouth, Cumberland, England. She was born in 1844 in Cockermouth, Cumberland, England. She died in Mar 1895 in Cockermouth, Cumberland, England.

vii. RUTH BIRKETT was born on 09 Feb 1841 in Cockermouth, Cumberland, England. She died in 1891 in Cockermouth, Cumberland, England.

14.   viii. DAVID BIRKETT was born in Jul 1838 in Cockermouth, Cumberland, England. He died on 27 Mar 1906 in Carbondale City,Lackawanna,Pennsylvania. He married (1) WILLHEMINA HESSE about 1871 in Pennsylvania,USA. She was born about 1849 in Pennsylvania, USA. She died on 24 Apr 1918 in Carbondale, Lackawanna, Pennsylvania. He married (2) ELIZABETH FERRYMAN on 11 Nov 1860 in All Saints Church,Cockermouth,England. She was born in 1836 in Cumberland, England. She died in 1865 in Cumberland, England.

15.   ix. JOHNSTON BIRKETT was born about 1828 in Cockermouth, Cumberland, England. He died on 05 May 1852 in Cockermouth, Cumberland, England. He married Ann Johnston on 17 Jun 1850 in All Saints Church,Cockermouth,England. She was born about 1828 in Hawkeshead,Lancashire,England. She died in 1887 in Cumberland, England.

16.   x. WILLIAM BIRKETT was born about 1826 in Cockermouth, Cumberland, England. He died on 03 Mar 1898 in Cockermouth, Cumberland, England. He married Elizabeth Hodgson in Sep 1847 in Cockermouth, Cumberland, England. She was born about 1823 in Maryport, Cumberland, England. She died in 1884 in Cockermouth, Cumberland, England.

17.   xi. ISAAC BIRKETT was born in 1825 in Cockermouth, Cumberland, England. He died on 15 Apr 1891 in Cockermouth, Cumberland, England. He married Jane Gorley in Jul 1843 in Cockermouth, Cumberland, England. She was born in 1822 in Cockermouth, Cumberland, England. She died on 23 Aug 1891 in Cumberland, England.

18.   xii. JOHN BIRKETT was born in 1833 in Cockermouth, Cumberland, England. He died on 06 Nov 1874 in Salter and Eskett,Cumberland,England. He married Grace Miniken on 18 Jan 1858 in All Saints Church,Cockermouth,England. She was born on 15 Oct 1840 in Cmouth, Cumberland, England. She died on 05 Apr 1916 in Main Street,Dearham,Cumberland.

4.   **JOSEPH**[2] **CRAGG** (Isaac[1]) was born on 04 Apr 1803 in Cockermouth, Cumberland, England. He

died on 02 Jul 1878 in Cockermouth, Cumberland, England (Acute Bronchitis). He married Hannah Grave, daughter of Henry Grave and Margaret, on 01 Dec 1823 in Brigham Parish, Cumberland, England. She was born on 20 Mar 1803 in Cockermouth, Cumberland, England. She died on 17 Jul 1878 in Cockermouth, Cumberland, England (Phthisis Pulmonalis). Joseph Cragg and Hannah Grave had the following children:

19.   i. HENRY³ CRAGG was born on 05 Mar 1827 in Cockermouth, Cumberland, England. He died on 17 Mar 1903 in King Street, North Botany, New South Wales, Austrailia (Broncitis & Exhaustion). He married Mary Ann Geddes, daughter of Alexander Geddes and Martha Taylor, on 01 Mar 1846. She was born in 1829 in County Tyrone, Northern Ireland. She died on 27 Apr 1868 in Waterloo, New South Wales, Australia.

       ii. JOHN CRAGG was born on 26 Jun 1832 in Cockermouth, Cumberland, England.

       iii. WILLIAM CRAGG was born on 20 Mar 1837 in Cockermouth, Cumberland, England. He died in May 1849 in Cockermouth, Cumberland, England.

20.   iv. ROBERT CRAGG was born on 10 Jul 1834 in Cockermouth, Cumberland, England. He died in Dec 1862 in Cockermouth, Cumberland, England. He married Eleanor Farrell on 27 Jul 1857 in All Saints, Cockermouth, Cumberland, Eng.

21.   v. HANNAH CRAGG was born in Jul 1845 in Cockermouth, Cumberland, England. She died in Sep 1909 in Cockermouth, Cumberland, England. She married George Booth, son of George Booth and Mary Booth, on 02 Jul 1876 in All Saints Church, Cockermouth, Cumberland, England. He was born in 1848 in Hunslet, Yorkshire, England. He died in Mar 1901 in Cockermouth, Cumberland, England.

22.   vi. JOSEPH CRAGG was born on 01 May 1829 in Cockermouth, Cumberland, England. He died on 15 May 1866 in Cockermouth, Cumberland, England. He married (1) SARAH JANE FLEMING, daughter of Robert Fleming and Agness, on 05 May 1850 in Clifton, Cumberland, England. She was born on 11 Mar 1829 in Whitehaven, Cumberland, England. She died in Sep 1889 in Cockermouth, Cumberland, England.

23.   vii. ISAAC CRAGG was born on 30 Jan 1825 in Cockermouth, Cumberland, England. He died in Jan 1894 in Westmorland, United Kingdom. He married (1) ANN SMITH on 14 Dec 1849 in Kendal, Westmorland, England. She was born about 1826 in Ireland. She died in Jan 1876 in Kendal, Westmorland, England. He married (2) ALICE BROADBENT in Oct 1881 in Lancaster, Lancashire, England. She was born about 1821 in Waddington, Yorkshire, England. He married (3) SARAH. She was born in 1832 in Worthington, Cumberland, England. She died in Cockermouth, Cumberland, England.

5. SOLOMON² CRAGG (Isaac¹) was born on 17 Mar 1809 in Cockermouth, Cumberland, England. He died on 06 Feb 1863 in Dearham, Cumberland, England (Cumberland Pacquet, and Ware's Whitehaven Advertiser - Tuesday 17 February 1863 pg 5. Dearham, on 6th inst, Mr. Solomon Cragg, aged 54 years). He married Elizabeth Hodgson, daughter of Henry Hodgson and Elizabeth Elliott, on 09 Jun 1832 in Bridekirk Parish, Cumberland, England. She was born on 07 Jul 1808 in Bridekirk Cumberland.

Solomon Cragg and Elizabeth Hodgson had the following child:

24.   i. ELIZABETH³ CRAGG was born in 1832 in Cockermouth, Cumberland, England. She married

(1) JOHN PEARSON. He was born about 1831 in Aglionby, Cumberland, England. She married an unknown spouse on 24 Jun 1855 in Carlisle, Cumberland, England (Carlisle Journal - Friday 06 July 1855 pg 8. Mr. John Pearson, commercial traveller of this city, to Miss Elizabeth Cragg, only daughter Mr. Solomon Cragg, of Dearham. At St. Cuthbert's Church, on the 3rd inst., by the Rev. A Marshall, M. A.).

6. **ELIZABETH**[2] **CRAGG** (Isaac[1]) was born on 24 Dec 1810 in Cockermouth, Cumberland, England. She died on 10 Jun 1875 in Cumberland, England. She married (2) **WILLIAM HODGSON**, son of Henry Hodgson and Elizabeth Elliott, on 25 May 1833 in Bridekirk Parish, Cumberland, England. He was born on 07 Oct 1804 in Tallentire, Cumberland, England. He died in Oct 1858 in Cockermouth, Cumberland, United Kingdom.

Elizabeth Cragg had the following children:

25. i. ISAAC[3] HODGSON was born in Jan 1839 in Brydekirk, Cumberland, England. He died in Mar 1898 in Cumberland, England. He married (1) JANE HODGSON. She was born about 1847 in Dearham, Cumberland, England. She died on 06 Dec 1885 in Carlisle, Cumberland, England. He married an unknown spouse in Oct 1861 in Cumberland.

ii. THOMAS HODGSON was born about 1848 in Dearham, Cumberland, England.

iii. WILLIAM HODGSON was born about 1842 in Standingstone, Cumberland, England.

iv. SARAH HODGSON was born about 1846 in Dearham, Cumberland, England.

v. JANE HODGSON was born about 1850 in Dearham, Cumberland, England.

vi. JOHN HODGSON was born about 1844 in Standingstone, Cumberland, England.

William Hodgson and Elizabeth Cragg had the following children:

i. RUTH[3] HODGSON was born in 1834 in Dovenby, Cumberland, England.

ii. BETSY HODGSON was born in 1835 in Standingstone, Cumberland, England.

26. iii. HENRY HODGSON was born in 1837 in Standingstone, Cumberland, England. He married (1) MARY A. HODGSON. She was born about 1847 in Ireby, Cumberland, England. He married an unknown spouse in Apr 1858 in Cumberland.

25. iv. ISAAC HODGSON was born in Jan 1839 in Brydekirk, Cumberland, England. He died in Mar 1898 in Cumberland, England. He married (1) JANE HODGSON. She was born about 1847 in Dearham, Cumberland, England. She died on 06 Dec 1885 in Carlisle, Cumberland, England. He married an unknown spouse in Oct 1861 in Cumberland.

v. WILLIAM HODGSON was born about 1842 in Standingstone, Cumberland, England.

vi. JOHN HODGSON was born about 1844 in Standingstone, Cumberland, England.

vii. SARAH HODGSON was born about 1846 in Dearham, Cumberland, England.

viii. THOMAS HODGSON was born about 1848 in Dearham, Cumberland, England.

ix. JANE HODGSON was born about 1850 in Dearham, Cumberland, England.

x. MARY HODGSON was born in 1853 in Cumberland, England.

xi. SARAH HODGSON was born about 1856 in Bridekirk, Cumberland, England.

Generation 3

7. **RUTH³ CRAGG** (John², Isaac¹) was born about 1817 in Cockermouth, Cumberland, England. She died in 1901 in Cumberland, England. She married Henry Hodgson on 06 Aug 1836 in Cumberland, England. He was born in 1808 in Tallantire, Cumberland, England. He died in 1879 in Cumberland, England.

    Henry Hodgson and Ruth Cragg had the following children:

    i.   JOHN⁴ HODGSON was born in 1836 in Cumberland, England.

    ii.   ELIZABETH HODGSON was born in 1839 in Cumberland, England.

    iii. JANE HODGSON was born in 1839 in Cumberland, England.

    iv.   BETSY HODGSON was born about 1839 in Dovenby, Cumberland, England.

    v.   HENRY HODGSON was born on 25 Dec 1842 in Cumberland, England. He died in 1910.

    vi.   MARGARET HODGSON was born in 1846. She died in 1850 in Cumberland, England.

    vii. SARAH ANN HODGSON was born on 12 Oct 1846 in Dovenby, Cumberland, England.

    viii. ELINOR HODGSON was born in 1849 in Cumberland, England.

    ix.   ELLEN HODGSON was born in 1850 in Dovenby, Cumberland, England.

    x.   ELLIOT HODGSON was born in 1852 in Tallantire, Cumberland, England.

    xi.   JAMES HODGSON was born in 1857 in Papcastle, Cumberland, England.

    xii. RUTH HODGSON was born in 1860 in Papcastle, Cumberland, England. She died in 1939 in Cumberland, England.

8. **ELIZABETH³ CRAGG** (John², Isaac¹) was born on 28 Mar 1819 in Cockermouth, Cumberland, England. She died in Mar 1881 in Whitehaven, Cumberland, England. She married (1) **WILLIAM HODGSON**. He was born in 1804 in Cumberland, England. She married (2) **WILLIAM GRAVE**, son of Joseph Grave, on 19 Aug 1843 in All Saints, Cockermouth, Cumberland, Eng (At Cockermouth, on Friday the 18th inst., Mr. Wm. Grave, shoemaker, to Miss Elizabeth Cragg.). He was born about 1812 in Cockermouth, Cumberland, England.

    William Hodgson and Elizabeth Cragg had the following children:

    i.   HENRY⁴ HODGSON was born in 1838 in Cumberland, England.

    ii.   WILLIAM HODGSON was born in 1842 in Cumberland, England.

9. **SOLOMON³ CRAGG** (John², Isaac¹) was born on 03 Apr 1836 in Cockermouth, Cumberland, England. He died in Apr 1894 in Cumberland, England.

    Solomon Cragg had the following child:

    i.   SARAH⁴ CRAGG was born in 1869 in Cockermouth, Cumberland, England.

10. **THOMAS³ CRAGG** (John², Isaac¹) was born in Oct 1838 in Cockermouth, Cumberland, England. He married Susannah Digney, daughter of Bernard Digney and Mary, on 15 Feb 1858 in Cockermouth, Cumberland, England (vol 10b page 535). She was born in 1842 in Whitehaven, Cumberland, England.

    Thomas CRAGG and Susannah Digney had the following children:

       i.   SARAH[4] CRAGG was born on 17 Nov 1876 in Usworth, Durham, England.

      ii.   MARY J. CRAGG was born about 1870 in Cockermouth, Cumberland, England. She died on 22 Sep 1937 in Springwell Village, Tyneside, Tyne & Wear, England, UK. She married (1) JOSEPH CLARKE on 06 Dec 1884. He was born about 1864 in Egremont, Cumberland, England. He died between 1911-1916. She married (2) JOHN REYNOLDS on 27 Jul 1916.

     iii.   WILLIAM CRAGG was born in 1863 in Dearham, Cumberland, England. He married Mary Ann Smith on 12 Sep 1882 (Roman Catholic). She was born in 1864 in Stavley, Derbyshire, England.

11.   **JOSEPH[3] BIRKETT** (Ruth[2] Cragg, Isaac[1] Cragg) was born on 19 Jan 1823 in Cockermouth, Cumberland, England. He died on 17 Nov 1901 in Carbondale, Lackawanna, Pennsylvania, USA. He married (1) **SARAH J HEWITSON** on 15 Sep 1897 in Buffalo, New York, USA. She was born in Apr 1851 in Pennsylvania,USA. He married (2) **ANN DRUMMOND** on 26 Dec 1842 in All Saints Church,Cockermouth, England. She was born on 13 Mar 1823 in Cockermouth, Cumberland, England. She died on 19 Sep 1895 in Carbondale City,Lackawanna,Pennsylvania.

Joseph Birkett and Ann Drummond had the following child:

       i.   JAMES B.[4] NICHOLSON was born about 1861 in Pennsylvania.

12.   **THOMAS[3] BIRKETT** (Ruth[2] Cragg, Isaac[1] Cragg) was born about 1834 in Cockermouth, Cumberland, England. He died on 26 Dec 1894 in Carbondale City,Lackawanna,Pennsylvania. He married Helen Eliza Crocker about 1874 in Lackawanna,Carbondale,PA. She was born in Jan 1844 in Pennsylvania,USA. She died on 20 Nov 1916 in Carbondale, Lackawanna, Pennsylvania, USA.

Thomas Birkett and Helen Eliza Crocker had the following children:

       i.   ALBERT FREDERICK[4] BIRKETT was born on 11 Sep 1876 in Carbondale, Lackawanna, Pennsylvania, USA. He died on 19 Mar 1933 in Carbondale, Lackawanna, Pennsylvania, USA.

      ii.   SIDNEY G BIRKETT was born in Jun 1875 in Carbondale, Lackawanna, Pennsylvania, USA. He died on 08 Aug 1907 in Carbondale City,Lackawanna,Pennsylvania.

13.   **RICHARD[3] BIRKETT** (Ruth[2] Cragg, Isaac[1] Cragg) was born on 03 Jun 1843 in Cockermouth, Cumberland, England. He died in Jun 1915 in Cockermouth, Cumberland, England. He married Margaret Quin, daughter of William Quin and Ellen Queen, in 1865 in Cockermouth, Cumberland, England. She was born in 1844 in Cockermouth, Cumberland, England. She died in Mar 1895 in Cockermouth, Cumberland, England.

Richard Birkett and Margaret Quin had the following children:

       i.   ISAAC[4] BIRKETT was born in Mar 1876 in Cockermouth, Cumberland, England. He died in Jun 1956 in Nelson, Lancashire, England.

      ii.   RUTH BIRKETT was born in 1871 in Cockermouth, Cumberland, England.

     iii.   WILLIAM BIRKETT was born about 1868 in Cockermouth, Cumberland, England. He died on 14 Nov 1874 in Cockermouth, Cumberland, England.

     iv.   JOHN BIRKETT was born about 1867 in Cockermouth, Cumberland, England. He died on 22 May 1937 in Cumberland, England.

14.   **DAVID[3] BIRKETT** (Ruth[2] Cragg, Isaac[1] Cragg) was born in Jul 1838 in Cockermouth, Cumberland, England. He died on 27 Mar 1906 in Carbondale City,Lackawanna,Pennsylvania. He married (1)

WILLHEMINA HESSE about 1871 in Pennsylvania,USA. She was born about 1849 in Pennsylvania, USA. She died on 24 Apr 1918 in Carbondale, Lackawanna, Pennsylvania. He married (2) ELIZABETH FERRYMAN on 11 Nov 1860 in All Saints Church,Cockermouth,England. She was born in 1836 in Cumberland, England. She died in 1865 in Cumberland, England.

David Birkett and Willhemina Hesse had the following children:

- i. ALICE[4] BIRKETT was born in 1883 in Pennsylvania,USA. She died on 04 Oct 1929 in Carbondale City, Lackawanna, Pennsylvania.
- ii. ANNIE BIRKETT was born about 1871 in Pennsylvania,USA.
- iii. JOSEPH BIRKETT was born about 1873 in Pennsylvania,USA.

David Birkett and Elizabeth Ferryman had the following child:

- iv. MARGARET BIRKETT was born in 1862 in Cockermouth, Cumberland, England. She died on 18 Jan 1934 in Cumberland, England.

15. **JOHNSTON[3] BIRKETT** (Ruth[2] Cragg, Isaac[1] Cragg) was born about 1828 in Cockermouth, Cumberland, England. He died on 05 May 1852 in Cockermouth, Cumberland, England. He married Ann Johnston on 17 Jun 1850 in All Saints Church,Cockermouth,England. She was born about 1828 in Hawkeshead,Lancashire,England. She died in 1887 in Cumberland, England.

Johnston Birkett and Ann Johnston had the following children:

- i. RUTH[4] BIRKETT was born about 1853 in Cockermouth, Cumberland, England.
- ii. JOHN BIRKETT was born in Aug 1850 in Cockermouth, Cumberland, England. He died in Sep 1850 in Cockermouth, Cumberland, England.

16. **WILLIAM[3] BIRKETT** (Ruth[2] Cragg, Isaac[1] Cragg) was born about 1826 in Cockermouth, Cumberland, England. He died on 03 Mar 1898 in Cockermouth, Cumberland, England. He married Elizabeth Hodgson in Sep 1847 in Cockermouth, Cumberland, England. She was born about 1823 in Maryport, Cumberland, England. She died in 1884 in Cockermouth, Cumberland, England.

William Birkett and Elizabeth Hodgson had the following children:

- i. FRANCES BORTHWICK[4] BIRKETT was born in Mar 1868 in Cockermouth, Cumberland, England.
- ii. SARAH ANN BIRKETT was born in Sep 1850 in Cockermouth, Cumberland, England. She died in Mar 1901 in Cockermouth, Cumberland, England.

17. **ISAAC[3] BIRKETT** (Ruth[2] Cragg, Isaac[1] Cragg) was born in 1825 in Cockermouth, Cumberland, England. He died on 15 Apr 1891 in Cockermouth, Cumberland, England. He married Jane Gorley in Jul 1843 in Cockermouth, Cumberland, England. She was born in 1822 in Cockermouth, Cumberland, England. She died on 23 Aug 1891 in Cumberland, England.

Isaac Birkett and Jane Gorley had the following children:

- i. ROBERT[4] BIRKETT was born in 1847 in Cockermouth, Cumberland, England.
- ii. ISAAC BIRKETT was born in 1860 in Dearham, Cumberland, England. He died in 1857 in Cumberland, England.
- iii. SARAH BIRKETT was born in Dec 1852 in Cockermouth, Cumberland, England. She died on 17 Apr 1853 in Sullart Street,Cockermouth,Cumberland,England.
- iv. WILLIAM BIRKETT was born in 1863 in Dearham,Cumberland,England. He died on 05 Jul 1864 in Dearham,Cumberland,England.

v. GEORGE BIRKETT was born in Sep 1864 in Ellenborough, Cumberland, England. He married AGNES MCDOUGALL. She was born on 23 Mar 1865 in Dornock, Dumfries, Scotland.

vi. JOSEPH BIRKETT was born in 1859 in Dearham, Cumberland, England.

vii. THOMAS BIRKETT was born about 1857 in Ellenborough, Cumberland, England. He died in 1942 in Cockermouth, Cumberland, England.

viii. JOHNSTON BIRKETT was born in Jun 1854 in Cockermouth, Cumberland, England. He died in 1928.

ix. ISAAC BIRKETT was born in 1861 in Dearham,Cumberland,England. He died in 1936 in Cockermouth, Cumberland, England.

x. ANN BIRKETT was born about 1850 in Cockermouth, Cumberland, England. She died in Mar 1867 in Cumberland, England.

xi. JOHN BIRKETT was born in Jan 1844 in Cockermouth, Cumberland, England. He died on 24 Dec 1926 in Cockermouth, Cumberland, England. He married ANNE BICKETT. She was born in 1841 in Sunderland, Cumberland, England.

18. JOHN[3] BIRKETT (Ruth[2] Cragg, Isaac[1] Cragg) was born in 1833 in Cockermouth, Cumberland, England. He died on 06 Nov 1874 in Salter and Eskett,Cumberland,England. He married Grace Miniken on 18 Jan 1858 in All Saints Church,Cockermouth, England. She was born on 15 Oct 1840 in Cmouth, Cumberland, England. She died on 05 Apr 1916 in Main Street,Dearham,Cumberland. John Birkett and Grace Miniken had the following children:

i. THOMAS[4] BIRKETT was born in 1869 in Cockermouth, Cumberland, England. He died in 1908 in Cockermouth, Cumberland, England. He married Margaret Ann White on 16 Apr 1892 in Keswick, Cumberland, England (Congregational Chapel, Keswick, England). She was born about 1871 in Keswick, Cumberland, England.

ii. MARY BIRKETT was born about 1863 in Cockermouth, Cumberland, England.

iii. JOHNSTON BIRKETT was born in Dec 1860 in Cockermouth, Cumberland, England. He died in 1862 in Cockermouth, Cumberland, England.

iv. ISAAC BIRKETT was born in Dec 1858 in Cockermouth, Cumberland, England. He married Sarah Postlethwaite on 23 Oct 1886 in Keswick,Cumberland,England. She was born about 1865 in Keswick,Cumberland,England. She died in 1917 in Cumberland, England.

v. ALFRED BIRKETT was born on 14 Nov 1870 in Crown Street,Cockermouth,Cumberland. He died in 1889 in Carlisle, Cumberland, England.

vi. JOHN BIRKETT was born in 1875 in Frizington,Cumberland,England. He died in Jan 1956 in Lanchester,Co.Durham,England. He married Elizabeth Ann Carter on 18 Jul 1896 in St Paul's Church,Winlaton,Co.Durham,England. She was born on 16 May 1876 in 3 Boundary Street,Newcastle Upon Tyne,England. She died on 24 Feb 1966 in Co.Durham,England.

19. HENRY[3] CRAGG (Joseph[2], Isaac[1]) was born on 05 Mar 1827 in Cockermouth, Cumberland, England. He died on 17 Mar 1903 in King Street, North Botany, New South Wales, Australia (Broncitis & Exhaustion). He married Mary Ann Geddes, daughter of Alexander Geddes and Martha Taylor, on 01 Mar 1846. She was born in 1829 in County Tyrone, Northern Ireland. She died on 27 Apr 1868 in Waterloo, New South Wales, Australia.

Henry Cragg and Mary Ann Geddes had the following children:

    i.   JOHN[4] CRAGG was born in 1853 in Cockermouth, Cumberland, England. He died in Jan 1855 in Cockermouth, Cumberland, England.

    ii.   JOSEPH HENRY CRAGG was born on 23 Jan 1847 in Cockermouth, Cumberland, England. He died on 18 Jan 1923 in Redgate, Riverstone, NSW, Australia. He married Mary Anne Jarman, daughter of Henry Jarman and Mary Santer, on 04 Feb 1868 in Free Church of England, SYDNEY, AUSTRALIA. She was born on 22 Sep 1844 in Redfern, New South Wales, Australia. She died on 18 Jul 1911 in Redgate, Riverstone, NSW, Australia.

    iii.   MARTHA CRAGG was born on 27 Jul 1851 in Independant Chapel, Cockermouth, Cumberland, England. She died on 31 Jul 1919 in Botany, New South Wales, Australia. She married Charles John Moore, son of William Moore and Sophia Silcox, on 09 Oct 1867 in 41 Burton St.. Sydney Reg #869 (SMH Saturday 2 November 1867 On the 9th October, by the Rev. Dr. Bailey, of the Free Church of England, Brisbane-street, Mr. CHARLES MOORE, to MARTHA, daughter of Mr. HENRY CRAGG, both of Botany Road, Waterloo. Conducted at 41 Burton Street, Sydney.). He was born in Jun 1846 in Frome, Somerset, England. He died on 23 Sep 1935 in Botany, New South Wales, Australia.

    iv.   WILLIAM H CRAGG was born in 1849 in Cockermouth, Cumberland, England. He died on 25 Feb 1906 in Botany, New South Wales, Australia. He married Eliza Moore, daughter of William Moore and Sophia Silcox, on 23 May 1870 in 47 Burton St.,Sydney, NSW, Reg # 44. She was born in Jan 1851 in Rode, Somersetshire, England. She died on 26 Jul 1938 in Mascot, New South Wales, Australia.

    v.   ALEXANDER CRAGG was born on 11 Feb 1856 in Woodmass Yard, Cockermouth, Cumberland, England. He died on 21 Feb 1894 in Kew, Victoria. He married Julia Ann Barling, daughter of Joseph Barling and Elizabeth Hill, on 31 Mar 1880 in Christ Church Anlican Church, Geelong, Victoria. She was born on 07 May 1861 in Germantown, Victoria, Australia. She died on 06 Jul 1936 in Geelong, Victoria.

    vi.   HANNAH CRAGG was born on 11 Oct 1858 in Cockermouth, Cumberland, England. She died on 12 Oct 1915 in Albert St., St.Peters, NSW, Australia. She married (1) HENRY BRYAN in 1901 in St Peters, New South Wales. He was born on 22 Feb 1854 in Woolloomooloo, NSW, Australia. He died on 02 Jun 1891 in St Peters, New

South Wales. She married (2) WILLIAM MARSHALL B ELGRE, son of James Belgre and Jane Cook, on 07 Dec 1901 in Prim. Methodist Ch, Newtown, Sydney, NSW. He was born in 1858 in Sydney, New South Wales, Australia. He died on 05 Dec 1950 in Lidcombe State Hospital, New South Wales, Australia.

    vii.   RACHEL ADELAIDE CRAGG was born in Jun 1863 in Chippendale, NSW, Australia. She died on 12 Apr 1864 in Waterloo, New South Wales, Australia (scrofulous. Swelling of glands and ? Reg. Chippendale #2066).

    viii.   JOHN ROBERT CRAGG was born on 24 Aug 1866 in Bullinaming Street, Redfern, NSW. He died in 1867 in Redfern, NSW, Australia.

    ix.   MARGARET ANN CRAGG was born on 07 Apr 1861 in Botany Road, Waterloo

Estate, NSW, Australia. She died on 14 Oct 1908 in Callan Park Asylum for the Insane, New South Wales, Australia. She married (1) FRANCIS HENRY HAYES, son of Francis Hayes and Elizabeth Murray, on 18 Sep 1879 in Sydney, New South Wales (HAYES-CRAIG.-September 18, at Bethel House, George-street North, by the Rev. T. Gainford, Francis Hayes, eldest son of Francis Hayes, of Darling-street, Balmain, to Margaret Ann, youngest daughter of Henry Craig, of Wyndham Grove, Alexandria.). He was born on 11 Apr 1851 in Balmain, New South Wales, Australia. He died on 02 Dec 1913 in Artlett Street, Paddington,New South Wales (Heart Disease). She married (2) ARTHUR GITTOES, son of William Gittoes and Mary Hilder, in 1894 in Granville, New South Wales, Australia. He was born on 21 Sep 1858 in Glenmore, New South Wales, Australia. He died on 20 Dec 1929 in Redfern, New South Wales, Australia.

    x.   RICHARD CRAGG was born in 1863 in Sydney, New South Wales, Australia. He died in 1863 in Sydney, New South Wales, Australia.

20.   ROBERT[3] CRAGG (Joseph[2], Isaac[1]) was born on 10 Jul 1834 in Cockermouth, Cumberland, England. He died in Dec 1862 in Cockermouth, Cumberland, England. He married Eleanor Farrell on 27 Jul 1857 in All Saints, Cockermouth, Cumberland, Eng.

Robert Cragg and Eleanor Farrell had the following child:

    i.   ELIZABETH H.[4] CRAGG was born about 1867 in Leeds, Yorkshire, England.

21.   HANNAH[3] CRAGG (Joseph[2], Isaac[1]) was born in Jul 1845 in Cockermouth, Cumberland, England. She died in Sep 1909 in Cockermouth, Cumberland, England. She married George Booth, son of George Booth and Mary Booth, on 02 Jul 1876 in All Saints Church, Cockermouth, Cumberland, England. He was born in 1848 in Hunslet, Yorkshire, England. He died in Mar 1901 in Cockermouth, Cumberland, England.

George Booth and Hannah Cragg had the following children:

    i.   ELIZABETH HANNAH[4] BOOTH was born in 1880 in Cockermouth, Cumberland, England.

    ii.   SIDNEY BOOTH was born in 1882 in Cockermouth, Cumberland, England. He married JANE DEWSBURY. She was born in Jun 1884 in Crosby, Liverpool, England.

    iii.   MARY ELEANOR BOOTH was born in Jun 1884 in Cockermouth, Cumberland, England.

22.   JOSEPH[3] CRAGG (Joseph[2], Isaac[1]) was born on 01 May 1829 in Cockermouth, Cumberland, England. He died on 15 May 1866 in Cockermouth, Cumberland, England. He married (1) SARAH JANE FLEMING, daughter of Robert Fleming and Agness, on 05 May 1850 in Clifton, Cumberland, England. She was born on 11 Mar 1829 in Whitehaven, Cumberland, England. She died in Sep 1889 in Cockermouth, Cumberland, England.

Joseph Cragg and Sarah Jane Fleming had the following children:

    i.   WILLIAM[4] CRAGG was born on 11 Apr 1851 in Cockermouth, Cumberland, England.

    ii.   AGNES CRAGG was born on 27 Mar 1853 in Cockermouth, Cumberland, England. She married Henry Johnston in Oct 1876 in Cumberland, England. He was born in 1857 in Down, Ireland. He died in 1886.

    iii.   JOHN CRAGG was born on 25 May 1855 in Cockermouth, Cumberland, England. He died on 03 Jan 1928 in Newcastle Upon Tyne, Northumberland, England. He married (1) ISABELLA CRAGG, daughter of Robert Stewart and Esther Stewart, in

1880 in Northumberland County, England. She was born in Jan 1860 in Newcastle Upon Tyne, Northumberland, England. She died in Jun 1944 in Newcastle Upon Tyne, Northumberland, England. He married (2) ISABELLA F OSTER STEWART, daughter of Robert Stewart and Esther Hudson, on 19 Sep 1880 in St Andrews Church, Newcastle upon Tyne. She was born on 29 Dec 1859 in Newcastle Upon Tyne, Northumberland, England. She died in Jun 1944 in Newcastle Upon Tyne, Northumberland, England.

iv. SARAH HANNAH CRAGG was born on 21 Nov 1862 in Cockermouth, Cumberland, England. She died on 28 May 1934 in 13 Ledgate, Kirkintilloch, Dunbartonshire, Scotland. She married an unknown spouse in 1896. She married (2) JOHN KERR in Jan 1896 in Cockermouth, Cumberland, England. He was born on 02 Oct 1862 in Whitburn, West Lothian, Scotland. He died on 17 Jun 1947 in 61 Eastside, Kirkintilloch, Dumbartonshire, Scotland.

v. ROBERT HENRY CRAGG was born on 31 Mar 1860 in Cockermouth, Cumberland, England. He died in 1890 in Carrington Near Newcastle. He married (1) MARGARET HARDY, daughter of Robert Hardy and Jane, in Jul 1882 in Cockermouth District, Cumberland, England. She was born in Apr 1860 in Greet Clifton, Cumberland, England. She died on 24 Dec 1931 in 21 Jane Street, Workington, Cumberland, England. He married an unknown spouse in Jul 1882 in Cumberland.

vi. MARGARET JANE CRAGG was born on 08 May 1865 in Cockermouth, Cumberland, England. She died on 13 Mar 1928 in Cockermouth, Cumberland, England. She married (1) JOHN HAWORTH LAW in Jan 1886 in Cumberland. He was born about 1866. She married (2) GEORGE GRAHAM in 1886 in Cumberland, England. He was born in 1865 in Chapel Brow, Cumberland, England. He died in Jul 1893 in Cumberland, England. She married (3) JOHN CALLION, son of John Callion and Mary, in Jul 1899 in Cumberland, England. He was born in 1871 in Greysouthern, Cumberland, England (Greysouthen, Cumberland). He died on 13 Jun 1937 in Cockermouth, Cumberland, England.

23. ISAAC[3] CRAGG (Joseph[2], Isaac[1]) was born on 30 Jan 1825 in Cockermouth, Cumberland, England. He died in Jan 1894 in Westmorland, United Kingdom. He married (1) ANN SMITH on 14 Dec 1849 in Kendal, Westmorland, England. She was born about 1826 in Ireland. She died in Jan 1876 in Kendal, Westmorland, England. He married (2) ALICE BROADBENT in Oct 1881 in Lancaster, Lancashire, England. She was born about 1821 in Waddington, Yorkshire, England. He married (3) SARAH. She was born in 1832 in Worthington, Cumberland, England. She died in Cockermouth, Cumberland, England.

Isaac Cragg and Ann Smith had the following children:

i. MARY ANN[4] CRAGG was born in Jul 1850 in Kendal, Westmorland, England. She died on 11 Mar 1923 in Fort William, Ontario, Canada. She married John Otway, son of John Otway and Mary Clifton, on 25 Jan 1873 in Westmorland. He was born on 02 Nov 1849 in Witherslack, Westmorland, England. He died on 11 Oct 1921 in Fort William, Thunder Bay, Ontario, Canada.

ii. JOHN CRAGG was born in Oct 1853 in Kendal, Westmorland, England. He died in Jan 1855 in Cockermouth, Cumberland, United Kingdom. He married EMMA CRAGG. She was born about 1853 in Kendal, Westmorland, England.

iii. HANNAH CRAGG was born in Oct 1855 in Kendal, Westmorland, England. She married Christopher Gibson in Jan 1873 in Westmorland. He was born on 18 Dec 1851 in Kendal, Westmorland, England. He died in 1896 in Kendal, Westmorland.

    iv.   WILLIAM CRAIG was born about 1858 in Alston, Cumberland, England.

    v.   JOHN S. CRAIG was born about 1865 in Alston, Cumberland, England.

Isaac Cragg and Sarah had the following child:

    vi.   JOSEPH WILLIAM CRAGG was born in 1860 in Cockermouth, Cumberland, England. He married an unknown spouse in Oct 1883 in Cockermouth, Cumberland.

24.   ELIZABETH³ CRAGG (Solomon², Isaac¹) was born in 1832 in Cockermouth, Cumberland, England. She married (1) JOHN PEARSON. He was born about 1831 in Aglionby, Cumberland, England. She married an unknown spouse on 24 Jun 1855 in Carlisle, Cumberland, England (Carlisle Journal - Friday 06 July 1855 pg 8. Mr. John Pearson, commercial traveller of this city, to Miss Elizabeth Cragg, only daughter Mr. Solomon Cragg, of Dearham. At St. Cuthbert's Church, on the 3rd inst., by the Rev. A Marshall, M. A.).

John Pearson and Elizabeth Cragg had the following child:

    i.   ANDREW⁴ PEARSON was born about 1857 in Carlisle, Cumberland, England.

25.   ISAAC³ HODGSON (Elizabeth² Cragg, Isaac¹ Cragg) was born in Jan 1839 in Brydekirk, Cumberland, England. He died in Mar 1898 in Cumberland, England. He married (1) JANE HODGSON. She was born about 1847 in Dearham, Cumberland, England. She died on 06 Dec 1885 in Carlisle, Cumberland, England. He married an unknown spouse in Oct 1861 in Cumberland.

Isaac Hodgson had the following child:

    i.   ISAAC⁴ HODGSON was born about 1882 in Dearham, Cumberland, England.

Isaac Hodgson and Jane Hodgson had the following child:

    ii.   WILLIAM HODGSON was born in Mar 1878 in Dearham, Cumberland, England. He died in 1951. He married JANE HODGSON. She was born in Jul 1880 in Dearham, Cumberland, England.

26.   HENRY³ HODGSON (Elizabeth² Cragg, Isaac¹ Cragg) was born in 1837 in Standingstone, Cumberland, England. He married (1) MARY A. HODGSON. She was born about 1847 in Ireby, Cumberland, England. He married an unknown spouse in Apr 1858 in Cumberland.

Henry Hodgson and Mary A. Hodgson had the following child:

    i.   GEORGE C.⁴ HODGSON was born about 1870 in Bothel, Cumberland, England.

Index

poacher, 56
tanner, 53, 54, 60
Cragg, Isaac (1805-1806), 47
Cragg, Isaac (1821-?), 68, 69, 70, 71
Cragg, Isaac (1825-1894), 77, 80, 97
Cragg, Jane (1799-?), 47
Cragg, Jane (1829-?), 68
Cragg, John (?-?), 12, 22, 23, 24
Cragg, John (1795-1849), 47, 63, 67, 68, 70, 72, 73
Cragg, John (1826-?), 68
Cragg, John (1832-?), 77, 80, 97
Cragg, John (1853-1855), 111
Cragg, John (1855-1928), 65, 108
Cragg, Joseph (1803-1878), 47, 77, 79, 83, 87, 95, 97, 98, 100, 108, 109
Cragg, Joseph (1829-1866), 77, 97, 98, 100, 108
Cragg, Joseph Henry (1847-1923), 111, 113
Cragg, Martha (1851-1919), 111
Cragg, Mary (1794-?), 47
Cragg, Robert (1834-1862), 77, 97
Cragg, Robert Henry (1860-1890), 108
Cragg, Ruth (1765-1849), 63
Cragg, Ruth (1801-1870), 25, 47
Cragg, Ruth (1817-1901), 68, 72
Cragg, Sarah (1783-?), 22
Cragg, Sarah (1832-1843), 68, 72
Cragg, Sarah Hannah (1862-1934), 108
Cragg, Solomon (1809-1863), 47, 63
Cragg, Solomon (1836-1894), 68
Cragg, Thomas (1838-?), 68, 73
Cragg, William (1837-1849), 77, 97
Cragg, William (1849-1906), 111, 113
Cromwell, Oliver, 5, 37, 38
Crosthwaite, 12, 20, 21, 22, 23, 24
Crosthwaite Parish Church, 12, 21
Cumberland Pacquet, 89, 90, 92
Cumberland, Duke of, 32
Currie, Captain, 91
Curwen family, 27, 28, 29, 81
Dalston, 89
Davison, Reverend Portas Hewart, 78, 107
Dearham, 24, 65

Dent, John, 48
Denwood, John, 100
Derby, Lord, 98, 102
Derwent, 44
Derwent Water, 14
Derwent, River, 10, 14, 29, 35, 37, 38, 39, 40, 42, 44, 54, 55, 57, 58, 60, 68, 69, 79, 95
Dickinson, William, 53
Digney, Susannah, 73, 74
Donaldson, George, 71
Double Mills, 80
Douglas, Earl of, 37
Dow, Neale, 96
Durham, Diocese of, 7
Eaglesfield, 6, 85, 96
Earee, Rev. William, 97, 109
Edward I, 41
Edward II, 36
Edward III, 43, 49
Egremont, Earl of, 37, 41, 53, 64, 82
Elliot, John, 90
English Civil War, 37
Fawcett, Rev Edward, 49, 60, 68, 82, 83, 84, 85, 90, 92, 94, 111
Fearon, John, 90
Fell, William, 85
Fielden, John, 86
Fife, Earl of, 37
Fisher, John, 84, 90
Fleming, Daniel, 23
Fleming, George, 100
Fleming, Sarah (1829-1889), 108
Fleming, Sir Daniel, 23
Fletcher, Henry, 37
Fletcher, Sir George, 44, 51
Fotheringhay Castle, 37
Fox, Samuel, 85
Free Traders, 98
Gaddis, John (1823-1894), 115
Galloway, Lord of, 37
Garley, John, 56
Gascoyne, Isaac, 85
Gatley, Reverend Edward, 78
Gaveston, Piers, 36

Steel, Thomas, 45
Stevenson, Robert Louis, 38
Steward, John, 85
Stewart, Randolph, 83
Stoddart, William, 80
Stuart, Charles Edward, 32
Swain, William, 100
Tannery, 58
Taylor, Martha (1803-1880), 113
Temperance Movement
  Band Of Hope, 96
  Good Templars, 96
  Rechabites, 95, 96
Thomlinson, Isaac, 94
Thompson, H., 68
Thursby, James, 94, 100
Thursby, John, 94, 100
Thursby, Thomas, 100
Tiffin, Joseph, 65
Tory Party, 82, 85, 98, 102
Tyson, John, 65
Umfranvilles, 41
Vikings, 12, 71
Viscount Garlies. *See* Stewart, Randolph
Wallace, William, 37
wallers, 67
weavers, 68, 80, 81, 83, 86, 87, 92, 93
Weight, George, 94
Westmoreland, 7, 9, 13, 17, 34, 122, 124

Westmorland, 5, 18, 23, 51, 67, 71, 80, 92, 93, 114, 117
Westmorland Gazette, 56
Wharton, Joshua, 80
Wharton, Philip Lord, 44, 51
Whig Party, 83, 84, 85, 87, 97, 98
Whitehaven, 28, 35, 45, 62, 73, 83, 89, 115
Whitehaven Gazette, 56
Wigton, 45, 89
Wilkin, Henry, 100
Wilkinson, Isaac, 100
Wilkinson, James, 100
Wilkinson, John, 94
Wilkinson, Jonathan, 68
Wilkinson, Joseph, 90
Wilkinson, William, 100
Wilson, Thomas, 94
Winder, Elizabeth, 46
Winscales, 31
Word, Jonathan, 45
Wordsworth, William, 10, 34, 38, 50, 51
Workington, 23, 24, 26, 27, 28, 29, 30, 31, 35, 45, 53, 61, 62, 96
wrestling, 71
Wybergh, Rev. Christopher, 84
Wybergh, Thomas, 56
Wyndham, General Henry, 60, 97, 104, 105
Wyndham, George O'Brien, 97
Yorkshire, 2, 7, 9, 92, 93, 118

www.ingramcontent.com/pod-product-compliance
Lightning Source LLC
Chambersburg PA
CBHW080847270326
41934CB00013B/3230